INTELLECTUAL MYSTICISM

INTELLECTUAL MYSTICISM

Ben Sheiner

Philosophical Library
New York

Contents

INTELLECTUAL MYSTICISM

INTELLECTUAL MYSTICISM

Once in a while there is a flash, a transitory glimmer of light that reveals, and what it reveals makes me gasp and then I'm saddened by what I am.

The flash reveals. I am saddened by what I am, but gladdened by what I shall yet be. The mystic lights of being flood my soul and I fuse into changing vibrations moving to eternity.

Around the core, the center of all being, dance and intermingle energies, divine pulsations thrust and intertwine. Vibrations fill and oscillations throb outward as the energies expand.

These energies are the center, the core of all Living. These energies are the pure contents that urge all of Life. These oscillations number *seven*. Their dance was set in Heaven and with infinite variety they move and change, shifting in their intensities, changing in their colors, reacting and moving, urging to expansion—to goodness and to beauty—urging on to motion, the motion of all of Life.

And about the core spinning like planets about the sun, spinning like electrons about the nucleus, twirl paired modifiers reflecting or deflecting—intensifying or dampening the energies from within. The modifiers number seven, too.

They twirl and whirl about the center. They glide and slide about the core. The light shines through according to their whirl. According to their twirl do the energies of Life expand. According to their changes does the content move within.

And if the rays of power are deflected, and if the pulsations are dejected and the streams of light darkened, then the energies fail to

The Key

MATERIAL		MATERIALISM	
PHYSIOLOGIC		UNPHYSIOLOGIC	
SEX		ANTISEXUAL	
LOVE		HATE	
COMMUNICATION		NONCOMMUNICATION	
CREATIVITY		DESTRUCTION	
IMMORTALITY		MORTALITY	

CORE FORCES   THOUGHT PRISON

2

The Key

HONESTY		DISHONESTY	
CURIOSITY		LACK OF CURIOSITY	
EFFICIENCY		INEFFICIENCY	
COOPERATION		COMPETION	
IDENTITY		ALIENATION	
PLEASURE		PAIN	
TRUST		FEAR	

POSITIVE BAG CONTENTS		NEGATIVE BAG CONTENTS	
LEADS TO		DOESN'T GO	
BEAUTY		UGLINESS	
UNDERSTANDING			
GOODNESS			

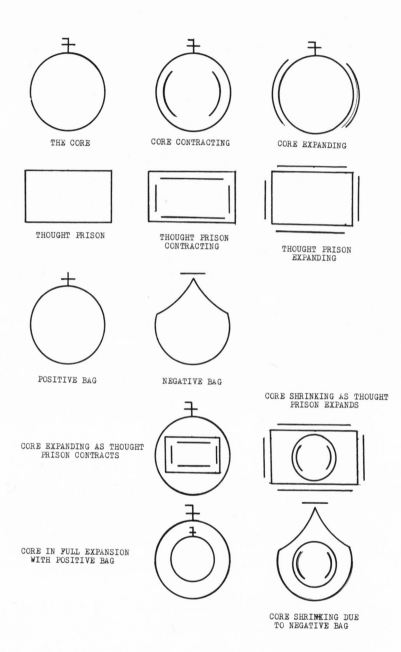

THE CORE

CORE CONTRACTING

CORE EXPANDING

THOUGHT PRISON

THOUGHT PRISON
CONTRACTING

THOUGHT PRISON
EXPANDING

POSITIVE BAG

NEGATIVE BAG

CORE SHRINKING AS THOUGHT
PRISON EXPANDS

CORE EXPANDING AS THOUGHT
PRISON CONTRACTS

CORE IN FULL EXPANSION
WITH POSITIVE BAG

CORE SHRINKING DUE
TO NEGATIVE BAG

expand. The dance slows in tempo. The lights lose their glimmer. They glow ever dimmer. Slowly they go out. The being ceases to be.

And if the rays of power are reflected, and if the pulsations are ejected and the streams of light lightened, then the energies succeed in expansion. The dance intensifies in tempo. The movement becomes more flowing. The lights gain in glimmer. They glow and shimmer. Rapidly they move out. The being increases in being. Awesome variety takes over as the steps move to the music, the orchestration of all being, in harmony and in accord to the laws of nature—the rules for infinite motion beyond all commotion, the way of true being, the way of God.

When the perceptions are honed and divinely inspired, moved and fired by the love of God, when the perceptions are filled with gentle pulsations divinely inspired by the trust in God, then the plan unfolds with all its magnificent glory and ecstasy fills the heart.

Visions, floods of lights, dreams to speed and fire, prophecies thrill before the mind. The body glows with the light and lifts the mind to ever greater levels. The being expands and in the expansion follows the way, the way of nature, the way of God.

Gather all you who would believe. Gather all you who disbelieve. Gather all doubters, cynics, scorners, haters and mourners. Gather all you crippled varieties of Life. Gather and use the reason to expand the soul.

There is a pattern to all of being from the most low on up. There is a pattern and there is a way to move up. Understanding is the key to all being. Unlock the mind and the soul flows out. *Unlock the thoughts and you will perceive.*

Thought Prison

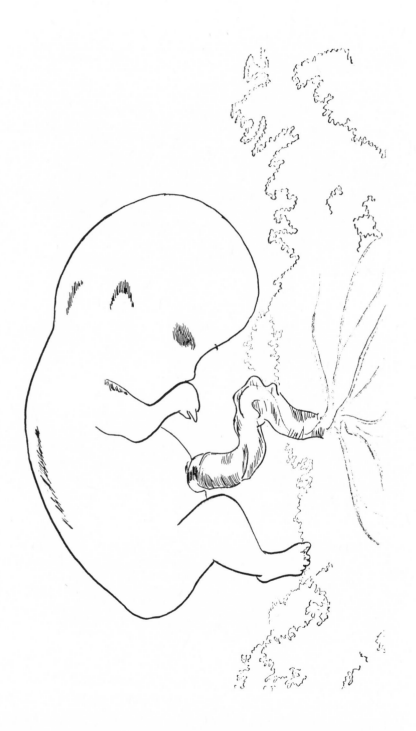

Physiologic ♂♀

Unphysiologic

SONG OF PHYSIOLOGY

The song of physiology is a song of being, a song of adaptation, of evolution, a song of demand. The biologic organism strives to be and in the striving it changes, changes, modifies and moves into different realms of being.

Atoms in stages of excitation coalesce and form molecules. Molecules move together to form cells. Cells form organs. And a whole is created. Newer, more complex beings come into being. Beings are created which are capable of finer perceptions, more varied movements, better able to respond to the environment, better able to be free.

The environment puts demands upon the structures and the changing patterns of structure exert influences upon changing patterns of function. The environments exert demands and those demands themselves change the environment. The evolving Life forms reactions and in the reaction the environment is modified.

The song of physiology is a song of being, and the song of being is a song of life. Energy moves from electron to electron, from molecule to molecule, from cell to cell. Energy moves and is amplified. Complex reactions take place. In a series of electronic states excitation grows. Varied vibrations occur dancing in varied wave lengths, bringing about excited states creating stronger and stronger reactions upon their neighbors—molecules—cells —organs—and beings. Electricity moves and Life is modified. It changes.

Electricity moves and Life expands. The electricity grows. Life expands. The changes become greater. Life accelerates and modifies. It expands, moves forward. And cells differentiate. Organs specialize. Individuals become varied. The differences excite. And Life moves forward in pulsating throbs.

Vibrational levels between and among molecules and cells, cells and organs, organs and beings, beings and society overlap and mix, amplify and move into higher lying electronic states. Each unit radiates and sends forth emissions. The inter-system crossing excites. The Life intensities increase.

The song of physiology is a song of Life, and in Life units need each other in order to grow. They need each other to interact, to expand, to change and be stronger.

The more complex the unit, the more capable it is of exerting energy, of modifying itself and others, of reaching levels of greater vibration. The more the individuals react, interact, move together and apart, the more their energies become amplified, the more they expand into greater levels of being.

With an increase of energy, finer motions are capable of being made, more intricate reactions can take place, more delicate perceptions can be obtained. The stores of information expand. The useage of information grows. Cycles of power excite and move in ever stronger currents.

People need people in order to be. People need people as sources of energy. People need people in order to free the potentials of Life within them.

The oscillations of the Life force are the movement of communication. The vibrations of Life depend upon the ease of communication and whatever impedes communication hinders the flow of messages, the currents of electricity—of excitation, movement and change.

To impede is to hinder. To hinder is to slow down. To slow down is to decelerate. The end is entropy—no energy at all!

Life is movement, change, modification, differentiation, increasing energetic states of being, states of interaction, action and counteraction. Life is movement towards a harmonious state of expansion.

11

The song of physiology is a song of Life. Whatever interferes with the physiologic processes interferes with Life. And good and evil become reduced to their simplest, most easily understood, thought complexes.

What is good must be good for being. What is good must be in harmony with Life increasing the vibrations, the electric oscillations moving forward to greater states of excitation—moving forward to greater energies, to higher levels of being.

What is evil impedes the flow. What is evil brings discord, a lack of harmony to the forces for Life, a poverty in being, decreasing the energies, winding downward into confining states of being, moving into states of weakened energies, attenuated states of being, bringing to death.

What is good for Life is good, is beautiful. What is good excites. What is evil decreases life, impedes motion, energy exchange. What is evil leads to poverty in being. It leads to death.

What is good leads to a longer and more energetic life. What is bad leads to a shorter less energetic life.

Integrated energies are energies in harmony with being. They make for the efficient transmission of information. They move to increased knowledge, increased perceptions and increased being. Integrated energies sing together, they sing for Life. Like tuning forks in a magnetic field, the increased harmonious vibrations set waves of electricity flowing, waves which change the environment and lead to greater electronic flow. Integrated vibrations increase energies. Increased energies increase Life. Moving waves of motion, action on to Life!

Motion is movement and movement depends upon differences in time and space. Differences excite to movement. It is the differences between individuals which lead to the greatest exchange of information and knowledge, which lead to the greatest learning. It is the differences that make communication most beneficial to those involved, which open up new vistas of perception, new potentials in being and in doing. Action on to Life!

The same continued stimulation eventually fails to evoke a

response. The stimulation depends upon differences. The differences tend to excite. The variety tends to ignite moving the imagination to demand exploration, moving to adventure, excitement, moving to more Life. Moving motion waves of action, action on to light!

The song of physiology is a song of vibrations, intermittent pulsations increasing in Force. The blood must nourish, the messages must flourish, the information must grow. Ignorance is poverty. Confusion moves to death.

The heart beats pulsations of warmth, Life giving sustenance, throughout the cells. The heart beats out throbs of energy to every organ system of the body. Its beat influences each and every cell, and each and every cell influences the condition of the body as a whole. Where the blood fails to flow adequately, cells shrivel and eventually die. Actions waves move to Light.

The song of physiology is the song of the heart beat, the song of warmth and energy, the song of pulsations full of Life. The song of physiology is a song of movement, of oxygen moving in and out, of carbon dioxide moving out and in. It's a song of difference, a song of exchange. Light waves of action, motion of delight!

The cells carry out their functions and in return place demands upon the environment. They must have nutriments. They must get rid of their wastes. They must have an exchange of gases. They need a temperature most optimum for their function. And their function is determined greatly by environment. Cell and environment feed back into each other and interact. Motion! Motion! Action waves of light!

Where the flow is adequate the function is most efficient. Where the environment places demands the cell grows to increase its abilities, its powers to do and interact. Muscles increase in size. Neural connections are opened up to increase the cerebral flow of electricity. Nerves and muscles grow stronger. Demands increase. Expansion occurs. Inertia for beneficial motion comes into being. Life expresses itself in a finer, greater, stronger, more creative being. Motion! Movement! Action waving on!

13

Inner stimulation demands outward stimulation, too. The flow of messages within demands a flowing out of messages, too. The greater the motion, the greater the action. Function influences structure and structure influences function.

Life strives to be only in its most primitive form. Life strives to expand beyond that point. In an inadequate environment each unit will compete even if it must do harm to its neighbor. Each unit will compete and in the competition eventually cause the destruction of the whole.

Competition is a primitive force for existence in a poor environment of scarcity, inadequacies, and demands exceeding capabilities. It's a short-range force for life. The cell merely prolongs its existence but eventually contributes to its own demise.

Cell depends upon cell neighbor. Its neighbor's well being increases its own. The strength of its neighbors strengthens it too. Action! Interaction! Motion of Might!

Cooperation is the key to harmony, the key on which physiology must sing. Cooperation strengthens but competition weakens and destroys. It makes for discord. It makes for noise.

Coordinated energies all in accord, surging messages reacting in warmth, increasing demands causing interactions, all this increases the tempo—the Life Force for being. Energy yielding processes must be coherent, coordinated and concentrated, in tune with the desires. They must be true to the beat of the heart.

The foundation of physiology is energy and energy makes for motion. The demand on physiology is for function, function for the creation of energy, for the perception of impulses, for the transmission of messages making for movement—reaction, action, waves of motion and interaction, waves for Life. The waves are patterns. They must be expanding patterns changing prevailing conditions, bringing to new potentials, exciting, firing, inspiring. Evolution is the way for Life. Life once set in motion strives always to evolve. Action! Action! Waves of motion, moving through to Light!!

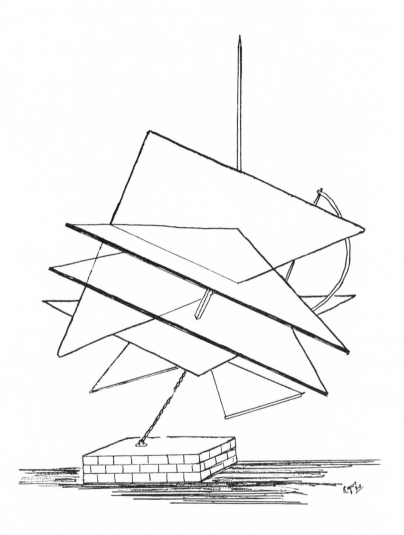

Material

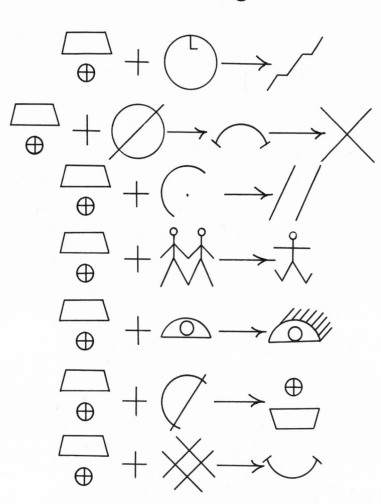

Materialism

SONG OF THE MATERIAL

Man has material needs. He needs shelter and clothing. He needs things to improve his physical existence. He needs devices for improving his powers of mobility and communication. He has need of invention.

Man needs inventions to evolve into a creature more capable of perception and abilities to do. Inventions amplify his sensory mechanisms. Inventions amplify his motor functions. They enhance and make possible a creature capable of journey into space.

Man enjoys beauty. He enjoys creation. Therefore he enjoys transforming his environment into a place of greater beauty, greater comfort and greater stimulation for himself. He elaborates upon his material needs.

The infant has material needs, too. He requires a place to sleep, warm clothing to replace the wet, a room, a roof, an environment stabilizing the temperature. As he grows his abilities increase and with his increased range of motion and capabilities come an increase in needs, needs to be stimulated, needs to learn and things to use.

The child needs toys to satisfy and stimulate his imagination. He needs clothing to protect him as he explores. He needs balls and games to help him increase his motor abilities and his enjoyment in his own body. He needs them to help him be a more social creature.

The greater his increase of maturity, the more become his material needs to enhance, color, amplify his being, magnify his joys and aid him in moving forward in his range of being. Motors increase his range of motion. Telephones, telegraph, television increase his range of communication. Microscopes, telescopes, oscilloscopes increase his range of perception. The human being must expand.

Expand? Can the toddler learn to fly the jet? Can he understand the world of microbes, the universe of stars and planets? When the expansion ceases, maturity becomes arrested.

In life there is never a status quo. Life demands expansion or else atrophy sets in. The being diminishes and becomes less.

Fear arrests expansion. Dishonesty, too. And fearful, dishonest people displacing the forces within turn not to expansion of being, but to expansion of things, toys without meaning, toys with no purpose since they don't improve, don't help in abilities but often hinder and destroy.

When things become symbols valued not for meaning but for form, the things become destructive. And people who are fearful, dishonest and distrusting, people who are pain filled have an arrested awareness turning down to the point of self. Oriented to the superficial they find little meaning in the things they use. They use and remain hungry. They get more things and the hunger becomes stronger. They get more confused. People to them become equated with things and things with people. They use and abuse things and people. They abuse and use people and things. They manipulate and scheme. They lose the spontaneity, their joy in being. But with the decrease in being comes a decrease in perceiving and they never know how shrunken and shriveled their core has become. With awareness fading they know only pain, they deny and the ache of the void they try to drown with alcohol, drugs and more lies.

People have needs. They require things to aid in their maturing. They need people to make them vibrate more intensely. They need guides, gentle leaders to emulate and imitate and to love. They need people for an exchange in knowledge. Things increase abilities but they don't fire, inspire and accelerate the warm energy of the core.

19

Arrested people get more pleasure out of things than they do from people. And the pleasure they get from things is so hideously superficial and the pleasure they get from people is so very small. Arrested people are joyless people, hungry people filled with empty ways, eventless days—craving—slaving but always moving down.

There are good things and bad things. Good is useful, Bad is useless, harmful and tends to hurt. Good excites. Bad provokes.

There are things which encourage, gladden the heart and fire to movement. There are things which discourage, sadden and slow.

For competitive people, how discouraging to be shown what is far beyond the ability to do. How discouraging to have one's efforts dwarfed and derided. How empty is the toy that fails to excite.

People need examples to emulate, to model themselves after, to imitate not to compete against. The desire to excel becomes confused with competition and the confusion makes unhappy, leads to conflict, leads to strife.

In confusion, useless things become valued, useful things destroyed. In confusion people turn to competition for incentive and beat each other down. The drive for material well-being becomes perverted into a drag, a rat race, an automatic reflex leading to decay.

Competitive people are disoriented from Life. They worship symbols without content. They are discontented inwardly while outwardly they pretend. The facade becomes all important. The front, the pretense, the lie becomes a fixed pattern and the environment becomes polluted with their ineffectual efforts to gain even a glimmer of pleasure.

The ooze of abuse clouds the vision contaminating Life. And this drive for form without content becomes called success. And success, this empty shell of being, becomes worshiped and it destroys. This empty shell of discontent, of hunger never fulfilled, becomes called materialism and confused with the material drive. The competitors compete for success and die bit by bit inside.

Their humanity gap deepens, widens. They suffer more and more and vent their frustrations in anger, aggression, hatred and war.

Man seeks to influence his environment and his drive for the material is part of the creative drive. The wise, the good, the mature try to better, improve and make more beautiful. Their efforts give them pleasure because their efforts are all good.

Men seek to change their environment. The qualities they possess are the qualities they project. The forces they use are the forces with which they surround themselves. And the environment, so changed, changes men for the better or for the worse. And the environment of fear, suspicion and pain is not an environment for a free flowing humanity.

Things that are not used are things which are wasted. Things that can't be used are things which are useless. Competitors are hoarders. They compete for things, things which they put away, keep in fear of future necessity. They place restrictions upon usage. They waste and make useless. And their attitudes toward things carry over in attitudes toward people.

The humanity gap widens. The sting of inner cold excites a gnawing hunger. They thirst for human warmth, and in confusion turn more and more to gadgets compounding their unhappiness. They fill the environment with their poverty and their poverty repels. The gaps between themselves and others, the voids of negativity whirl more viciously, hurt more severely and pain with an excruciating intensity.

Things not used efficiently are things not appreciated. People who don't communicate intimately are people not appreciated. Not to appreciate is not to enjoy. Materialism is a joyless state of mind.

Materialism is a symptom of arrested growth, a sign of fear, of misdirected energies, of a game directed away from Life. It's a drain of energies, an inefficient utilization of resources making for confusion.

An environment that encourages materialism is a distortion producing media. An environment that urges the use of the material towards advancement in doing and creating is an environment in harmony with nature. An environment that encourages materialism discourages sweetness, tenderness and love.

Man has need of invention, need of improvement, need of the material to spark his still greater needs for action. Action! Action! Waves of motion, moving on to light!

SONG OF SEX

Sex Song I

Sex is a direct expression of humanity, of life and of love, encouraging the generosity of the spirit and a true reciprocal sharing of total resources. It frees from regimentation. So powerful is its cohesive pull that it is the greatest unifying force for humanity, shaping the emotions into rockets for joy, forming the actions into movements for total creation.

Life ceases to be lived in a closed world. With sexual expansion the universe opens up and each opposite becomes a source of joy to the other. Deep feelings of love, common identity, and hopefulness spring into being. Transcending all coercive forces, expanding, maturing, evolving sexuality gives rise to spontaneous thoughts of pleasure and actions of joy spilling over, feeding back into every aspect of being. The entire being becomes pervaded with trust, a sense of identity, and a belief in the goodness of oneself and others. The unconscious forces shrink as the consciousness expands.

Through sex comes self revelation and self realization. One discovers and develops one's capacities to be of supreme satisfaction to others and thereby to infinitely increase one's own satisfactions. Through sex one arrives at an inner relatedness to mankind and an affirmation of life.

With an unfolding in sexuality comes an unfolding of the individual. It brings the conviction of being wanted, of being necessary, of being a source of pleasure and joy. It brings increasing happy images. It brings self-esteem and enhances dignity.

The emotional fulfillment coming with sexual fulfillment triggers cycles of expanding love, creation, communication and the very force for Immortality. It makes for a refreshing invigorating openness of action and thought, of reaction and being. It makes for a thorough enjoyment of the infinite movements of Life, an enjoyment which not only enriches the being but also tends to extend his very life.

Being expands and in the expansion neuro-electric currents flow in steadily in increasing streams making dreams into reality. Greater intelligence comes into being, the intelligence to penetrate, solve problems, direct energies and accomplish whatever a growing imagination can illuminate. Sex demands fulfillment and in fulfillment the being expands in every of the seven mystic stands.

Sex Song II

Sex is excitement, a movement for motion, harmony and accord, a play of emotion—pleasure sensuous and fine, a mixing of beings with love interchanged. It's warmth and embraces, kindness and smiles, the thrill of a touch and looks interchanged. The fragrance of life is inspired by total self-love.

Sex is a fire of many splendid flames, a desire for variety. It's beings merging in pleasure and touching souls, touching the heart of eternity. It's beauty and goodness, and all things adored in a heightened vision of loveliness.

Sex is the charm of creation, the fascination of movement, the wonder and awe of it all, a fabric of magnetic threads, the attraction for merging and refreshing the soul with vitality.

It changes configurations of habits and thought compelling modifications more in tune with life, tunes of joy and songs of love, melodies of living and of light. It charges the senses with receptions and makes aware of wondrous perceptions everywhere. Sex is healing, soothing and delight. It pulsates the being forward through every restraint enhancing the heart throb no matter how faint. It's an expression of love. It overcomes hate. It's an orderly pattern of varied design, a song of unfolding for all mankind.

It throbs with joy, open perceptions, happy receptions expanding the vision, sharpening learning, ever yearning for adventure and curiosity. It's a symphony of movement enhancing identity, feeding back information for ecstatic exchange. Sex moves to freedom. It moves to Love. It moyes to union. It moves to joy.

Sex is play moving the chemistries to greater reactions, moving the electro-magnetic attractions, enhancing the rhythms of the life flow, forcing the being to go and go. On to expansion, on to excitement, sex is a propelling fuel, a power for vitality.

It starts in the womb where it plays its tune as cells start to differentiate. It sounds ever stronger, forcing changes, modifications for identity. When the child is born in a more open environment, sex warms it, charms it and soothes its sensations, stimulating it on to growth, to increasing maturity.

Sex is part of the plan, an excitement of intricate design, a stimulating fabric woven of sparks, streams of happy beams of light moving forward to delight—moving on through eternity.

Between every molecule and every cell is this force for cohesive movement, coherent action of interweaving attraction giving meaning of magnification, building to a greater scheme. Sex moves to eternity. On wings of light and magnificent power sex streams through every cell causing pulsating union, a symphony of communication leading on to eternity.

Sex is an outpouring of glandular secretions, a formation of chemicals, molecules of pleasure. It enhances neural perception giving rise to amplifying molecules for magnifying being. Glands spurt. Impulses discharge. Nerves and muscles tremble and then relax. There's release and then the motion continues. Sex is tingling and warmth, cells flushed with pleasure, jetting streams of

Life. Sex is increased sensations. The Life Force grows. Hate and anger, fear and pain, all negations driven out by passion, passion for living and delight.

The fragrance of life is fired by total self love and in that self love sex is fulfilled. The senses of life are ever renewed, refreshed and filled with wonder and awe, filled with lucent crystal of color, vibrations of variety.

Sweet images, happy expectations of giving and receiving, of coming and going, fill the mind with causes for expansion. Total self-love spills over and over, organizes into an order of forward movement and merges to union, moves back again alone to gain further strength, energy for union once again. Moving sex is forward merger ever more splendid than before. So Life grows! Love grows! Sex sparks the way!

Enchanted by sensations into heightened realms of being we move on according to the messages we perceive. Signals internally connected and intertwined form structured patterns for receiving data systems for observations, abilities to correlate. The environment communicates with man and man communicates with it.

Sex clarifies and improves. It yields energy that changes, changes that move the perceptions, perceptions that move to growth. Sex improves the vision and the abilities to do.

Sex is a cycle for energy, amplification of being, waves of echoes and re-echoes, pulsations on for Life. Sex is neural discharges, patterns for perception, feedback ways of growing and maturing.

The greater the input, the greater becomes the potential output. The greater the input, the greater the energy within.

Sex is input, energy for Life, changes in physiological states, changes in chemical composition, changes for growth. Growth requires sex and sex makes possible more growth.

Sex is a force of communication. It's learning and teaching and the joy of both. It's a propelling force moving human to human, moving to gratification and beyond.

Sex is a flow of blood, and lymph, merging secretions giving

joy. It's a perfusion enhancing cells, a force for creation of memories.

Sex excites interests. It stimulates desires. It increases the abilities to attain pleasure. Sex is a treasure of Life.

Sex thirsts for variety and awareness. It broadens the tastes and increases experience. It's a force of nature always true.

Sex Song III

Sex is a drive for pleasure, a means of expressing joy. It's a desire for communion, a force for cooperation. It's the expression for Life.

Sex moves to maturity, a greater capacity for being and for doing, a greater ability to expand. Sex surges through the perceptions priming them for pleasure, moving them to excitement, urging them to Life.

Sex unlocks inhibitions permitting the free stream of urges—movements towards joy. It unlocks inhibitions and makes for a greater glow to our seeing, our very being, to our attitudes to Life.

The flames of Life flare more brightly, take on a vibrant glow colored by this force from heaven, this one force of the seven, this Sex Power Drive. The flames shoot up more strongly. They dance more intensely. They become more alive.

Sex releases blocks to communication. It paves the way to knowledge, fires human exchange. It makes for happy expectations, memory stores that glow with radiations eager to excite and set up electric vibrations extending from past to present and into the future too.

Sex is an ability to give pleasure and the ability to receive. It's the ability to attract and be attracted. It's the ability to perceive with all the neural connections working at top efficiency transmitting signals with expectation of joy.

Sex triggers energies for movement and interaction. It fires ecstatic impulses setting the soul into flight. Propelled with hones-

Antisexual

ty, it moves to greater being. Fired with honesty it roars stronger and more sure. Inspired by honesty it soars more pure to beauty and to the Divine. Receptors modifying and growing more fine, perceptions soar to higher levels of energy—stores of electricity vibrant and thrilling—inspiring onward in dancing flights of joy. Pure vibrant energies thrill the being, setting up patterns so merry and gay inspired by sex to dancing flights of joy.

Sex Song IV

Sex is a way of perceiving with color and excitement, with electro-magnetic strength. Sex is a way of thinking, cheerful and bright. It's a way of adventure, of gaining experience, a way of interaction, a human exchange.

Magnetic forces beam, vibrations stream and they attract. There's a movement together and then there's the throb. The motion moves outward and then the act repeats again each time with increased intensity. Vital vibrations follow shifting patterns moving on to eternity, gaining in meaning as they add to the being through increasing significant feedback helping define specific identity.

The strivings of sex are strivings for intimacy, strivings for identity and increased joys in being. The stirrings of sex are for interaction, for increasing abilities to give pleasure and to receive pleasure, too.

Sex is a way of gaining vigor, a way of broadening interests and unfolding life. Sex is a rhythm, a beat, the throb for creation and the blending of beings into fresh, new intricate ways.

Sex is a way of exciting the perceptions to the electromagnetic currents of variety, the infinite patterns of color and Life. Sex is a way of coloring the vision with pathways to the future, flowing designs of vitality. Sex sharpens, enhances, it moves to song. It bounces and dances, moving the soul along to infinity.

Sex is a way of consolidating the being into a more intense and

Sex

receptive individual capable of relating and caring. It is the trigger for discharging the individual into experiences of pleasure and growth. It is a power source capable of catapulting the individual into greater intensities of reactions and interactions, launching the individual into realms of excitement and adventure, moving to greater life—a life of charm and drawing together. It's a highway of verve, vivacity and imagination—an animation of creativity, enthusiasm and spirit. It's a way for joyous behavior, a revelation for needs to overcome inadequacies transforming the drab into a vivaciousness of delight for reciprocal sharing.

Sex is a prime mover of all emotions. Sex suppressed, sublimated, repressed or denied is sex distorted, forcing chronic frustrations, inner rage shaking apart the integrity of the individual throwing him into chaotic conflicts of emotion. Those who live in sexual poverty forever live with regrets and the emptiness of non-relating intimacy.

Sex is the oil for the biologic machine quickening its response to demand, demanding more response as it excites, exciting more demands as it responds.

The fruits of sex should be pure pleasure, colors brilliant and sweet filling life with beauty and memories to quicken the neuro-electric flow.

Sex is a way of experiencing the sweetness and loveliness in life. It's a way to greater capacities and greater happy demands, greater opportunities expanding life.

Sex Song V

Without self esteem there can be no true perceiving, no movement outward, no ability to love. Without self esteem the being shrinks inward, loses its capacity to dream, becomes a shell from which the soul retracts, becomes a facade, an empty lie.

The being aches, hurts, cries in pain, is full of confusion and full of strain. It moves to destruction instead of to life. It moves to dishonesties, clings to rigidities and cries in loneliness and strife.

Without self esteem all becomes darkened, dreary and dead.

Sex is a force for self esteem, a power to shake and stir the dream. It's a force to awaken into being reactions of purity, crystals of delight, creating differentiation, improving the sight. It soothes the hurt and makes clear that the pleasures of the Life come from the heart—the beat of organic creation that leads the orchestration in which the brain should take part in a harmony of sweetness, color, and cheer. It stirs and clarifies turning from fiction, turning from the artificial restrictions of man disoriented and confused. It stirs and brings together. It's a force for union, a force of cohesion to brighten the way.

Sex is a force for self esteem, a force for self love, a force for being and enhancing, a force for romancing all the other powers of life. Only when the self esteem is great enough can it spill over and radiate the warmth of love, giving and then receiving, setting into motion waves of self excitation capable of spontaneous movement beyond the orbit of the self.

All fantasy, all of dreams, all the actions of the individuals are ways to keep and hold to self esteem. That which diminishes or destroys, that which undermines and subtracts, must be oriented to death. The way to life is through self esteem. The electric currents flow through self esteem and the scheme, the dream, the plan unfolds. All of giving, all receiving, all of doing and creating, every breath of movement is meant to enhance the self esteem.

Sex is power. Sex is might. Sex enhances self esteem. Sex is force for delight, a force of pleasure made by God, a wondrous current for self esteem.

The soul can only throb with self esteem in pulsations, pure light and pleasure. So the soul moves out and so it dances in motions of union. The soul must have self esteem.

Sex is power and might, verve and delight, colorful sight and endless energy. It frees the being from restraint, frees the soul to pour forth in strains of pure melody.

Sex is self esteem, a way of viewing inward, a way of seeing outward, a way of pursuing the future in a burst of happiness. Sex must with love be intimately intermingled or it loses most of its powers for joy. Sex is love's fire, love is sex's desire. Together they form the backbone of all being, the essential nerve to the scheme, the essence of the plan.

Sex is self esteem, a way to dream of happier satisfactions yet to come. It's hope and desire made of softness and fire, made of moisture and flesh and a quest for union, made of a reaching up and a moving forth.

Sex is God's gift meant to be used, not to be abused, meant to be used for ever greater pleasure, never for pain. It's divine! It's fine! It's the spark for all creation, the trigger that sets the plan whirling into this expansive motion.

Sex is the expression of God's love. It's a force for humanity.

Sex Song VI

Sex is the power of being, being needed and wanting in return. It's the power of giving and getting, the force of blending and growing, of absorbing and fusing and springing back refreshed and full of vitality. Sex is a pleasure blended, made ever more splendid by love and experience.

Sex is the melody to cheer the feet, the movement of dancing feet floating on to improvement, greater capability. It's union and maturing. It's learning and teaching and expansion all the way. Sex is the tune that colors the beat, the force that moves to creation and on to eternity.

It's dreams, and streams of desire awakening and shaking to the awareness, to conscious knowledge and conscious seeking, to consciousness expansion and movement. It's the union of heart and mind, a blending of blood and nerves building up to explosive joys propelling ever outward, moving people to people out to joy.

To give and to receive and in the giving to set up waves of reverberant energies echoing and resounding is the greatest of all attainments. Sex is a force of prime motion, a force for devotion of all humanity. It's the unifying force for all.

Sex Song VII

Sex uplifts the emotions and surges forward the sensual abilities and range of potentials. It is the greatest of the liberating forces motivating and liberating the sexual self to move on to greater potentials of intimacy, of feeling and in abilities to please. It arouses and mobilizes forces for interaction based initially on self interest and the ability to act accordingly, maturing to an awareness of others and their needs. It leads to an enhancement of the pleasure principle governing life.

The exchange of biological satisfactions leads to an exchange of human warmth. It leads to an interaction of mutual benefit, mutual growth. It leads to a focus on others not as a means to an end, not as objects to be used and possibly be abused, but as an end in themselves. It makes aware in its unfolding that in others one attains one's pleasures. Through others one attains one's satisfactions. But most important of all, through the giving of enjoyment to others, one attains one's own greatest joys. This type of maturity makes most beautiful, most good and hence most holy.

Sex as it develops arouses greater desires which move into and strengthen the other strands of inner light. It is a natural intrinsic force for full development filling and bright. It relates individual to individual increasing awareness, consciousness and the intensities of interaction. It bestows feelings of increasing communion relating people to people to the world and the universe, too. It evolves into a relatedness to every single vibratory force, every single molecule, atoms and star. It relates individual to individual and individual to God.

Sex banishes loneliness, moves to cooperation, increases communication and leads to mutual stimulations. It gives meaning and

35

direction—the meaning of the relatedness to others—the direction of maximum satisfactions attained through the giving of satisfactions to others. It gives significance through the widening range of contacts and influences. Sex enhances the abilities to act.

The laws for sex are the laws of nature. The laws of nature forever concern motion, evolving, changing movement. Becoming ever more intense, movement outward, that's the law of evolution. The laws for sex follow the laws of nature. They follow the way of evolution—upward, outward, to greater movement—outward, upward to greater abilities to respond and to act.

It leads to greater freedom, a sense of emerging uniqueness. It leads to a union of self with the universe of stars and atoms—a union in the spontaneity of love and creation.

The concept of freedom changes according to the degree of one's awareness and conception of himself as an independent and separate being. It's a process of differentiation of the perceptions. Freedom has different meanings according to the stage of personal evolution, maturation, and awareness.

The abilities to differentiate are enhanced by education, experience, knowledge and information increasing abilities to respond and to do. The more the growth, the greater the quest for freedom and independence. And this quest is sparked by sex which leads to increasing abilities to differentiate.

Sex sparks growth; physical, emotional and mental growth. The spheres of growth are all integrated, an organized structure guided by will—a potential without end only when combined with honesty.

The process of differentiating the self from others, of increasing the fine perceptions, is a process of growing strength. It gives a new fresh way to relating ever evolving greater and greater.

Honest sex frees from coercion. It frees from restraints. It makes for a more intense maturity of closeness and solidarity of growing strength.

The more the individual becomes capable of differentiating himself from others, in noting the differences and enjoying the differences in the multi-varied vibrations about him—the greater become his capacities for freedom and the less of a reflex being he is. The adaptation to nature loses its coercive character. Man is the most adaptive, pliable and free to choose of all creatures.

Through sex man emerges from unconscious longings and stirrings to conscious fulfillment. Sex through experience brings about a pleasureable development of critical capacities. It thereby brings about a greater capacity for reason, greater spontaneous freedom in love and action.

Expanding sex leads to increased feedback information making for efficiency and beauty in movement. It expands the universe of self onto harmonious motion with others. As individuals discover others, so they also discover themselves. As they strive to bring pleasure to others, so they bring pleasure to themselves. Sex thus broadens the base of being adding stability, enhancing vigor.

Sex is a psychic need urging for expansion, for freedom to interact and through its fulfillment molds every aspect of personality and spirit. It increases strength, self reliance and confidence. It increases awareness, broadens vision and increases the inner capacity for faith. It frees the thoughts into moving patterns beneficial to self and to all of life and brings about the recognition that others are human sexual beings like the self. Growing sexuality teaches the significance of the self. It gives the self the direct ability to determine his own pleasure, change his environment, add to his experience by direct and purposeful actions. It makes for a fondness of self and of others. It makes for concern. It makes for involvement.

Sexuality unfolds into increasing initiative, the warmth of human self motivation to do good for self, for others, for God and universe. It leads to increasing independence, individuality and rationality. It increases skill of action, of discrimination, of intimacy. The individual expands in strength and warmth.

Health is the optimum of growth and happiness. Health requires, therefore, sexual expansion. No individual can be healthy, no part of his organism can fail but to suffer if the sexuality remains

37

restricted, constricted and repressed. Only with increasing sexuality can man give genuine expression, honest expression of his emotional, sensuous, and intellectual capacities overcoming the fictitious and irrational. With a thwarting of capacities toward expansiveness, sado-masochistic tendencies occur. People become oriented away from life instead of towards it.

Sex based upon equality and freedom becomes an expression of honest affection, and in the exchange becomes vibrant with love. The individuals involved are able to do what they want because they are properly aligned with the natural intrinsic forces of being. They seek to give pleasure to one another. Hence they succeed.

Sex turns to life, to the future. It turns to the miracle of creation, to that which has never been before. Honest sex is spontaneous and in the spontaneity it extends freedom, the freedom to be and to expand, the freedom to communicate intimately and effectively— the freedom for creation.

The surging power of sex lifts to freedom and independence where each stage in development leads to still greater potentials. It makes for a spontaneity and inner security from which one can venture forth with happy expectations.

The amount of destructiveness found in individuals is proportional to the amount that their expansiveness is curtailed, the blockage of spontaneity, of growth and of sensual, emotional and intellectual capacities. The life force then undergoes a degeneration into destructive patterns. Destructiveness then is the outcome of unlived life.

Every repression enforces the substitution of false feelings for the one that is repressed. Every repression detracts from the self, This substitution of the false for the original leads to the replacement of the original self by a facade suffocating the original, holding it prisoner, causing a loss of identity and feelings of insecurity and doubt. The self becomes an automaton falling back to repetitive narrowing cycles of behavior and action, giving up his spontaneous desires and creativity, giving up his humanity.

The false self fills up with hatred, anger, fear and all the negative emotions. It reacts reflexly and loses its abilities to carry out its intentions. It becomes filled with sado-masochistic drives interfering with honest appreciation and growth of pleasure. The sado-masochistic complex colors views of nature and of fellow-man. Both are seen as adversaries. It clouds the view of God Himself making Him appear an enemy. It fills with dread and turns to death.

Blockages to sexuality restrict spontaneity, inner growth and inner integrity. It causes antagonistic reactions which are suppressed along with the abilities to discriminate. Honest emotions become replaced with a cover of insincerity. This suppression of inner urges weakens the courage for spontaneous expression in all spheres.

Creative thinking and creative activity are inseparably linked with emotion. Poverty in emotions extends to poverty in thought and actions. The circle of intensifying joy and enthusiasm is lost through repressions which provoke fears and frustrations instead. The result is a flatness, a sterility, and a restlessness pervading existence with a tremendous underlying reservoir of fear and hostility. The result is an escape into insincerity and fictions.

All facts, information, and observations, must be approached with intense interest and passion, the same passion kindled by sex. Then knowledge becomes fired with excitement and thinking becomes a joy. Illusions vanish and the individual increases in strength. Strength is based upon inner integrity, an honesty in recognizing and admitting inner impulses. It's based upon Honesty.

It is the unfolding of sexuality that gives one the ability to trust in own capacities to think and to act. It is the heightening of the senses that increases awareness and permits a better perception of the relatedness of information and hence increases critical judgment. Pieces are correlated. They are seen to fall into a pattern. The puzzle is solved. The meaning of the whole becomes clear.

It is the unfolding of sexuality that gives meaning to being and authenticity. It brings self determination to actions. It brings a sense of identity. Each being becomes not limited to the feedback of a basic one or a few but expanded in the feedback of many. In this flow he is able to know and increases the self maturing, growing, increasing in abilities and in freedom of thought and action.

Through the freedom of emotions do thoughts expand the being into greater, fresher, more creative actions. Through the growth of joy does man move to greater spontaneous activity—activity motivated by the consciousness of inner desires in tune with the wondrous laws of nature. With spontaneity comes genuine happiness. In the spontaneous affirmation of self and others, in the union of man with the basic forces prompting him, comes meaning and fulfillment. In this spontaneous activity embracing the forces of life does the self grow strong and the soul expand.

Sex is an expression of the utmost affirmation of the self. The freedom of sexuality to grow is the freedom of individual affirmation making for the conscious awareness of innermost impulses, making for a unique movement of the soul through experience, interaction and the ever attainment of new potentials. With this growth of conscious inner awareness the unconscious fades and possibly will recede to a point where the soul will become conscious of the events of past lives just as in awaking we often retain the conscious memories of our night's dreams.

Sex is the trigger for initiative in cooperative adventure. It is the excitor of social humanity, shaping its energy to cohesive, constructive ends.

Spontaneous acts, acts of total freedom, are acts of abundance. Hence, the sexuality of abundance is a sexuality of freedom, generosity, tenderness and kindness fusing into love. It is the sexuality of abundance that makes clear the relatedness of each of the seven flames of the soul and reveals the awesome generosity of God whose cosmic intelligence fills the universe with order and motion holding true for all systems of creation.

The sexuality of abundance as an expression of human needs reveals a glimpse into the future generosity of humanity as they seek to mold themselves in total honesty in the image of their Creator. In this dynamic expansion of being do individuals intensify the intrinsic inherent divinity within their human nature.

Love

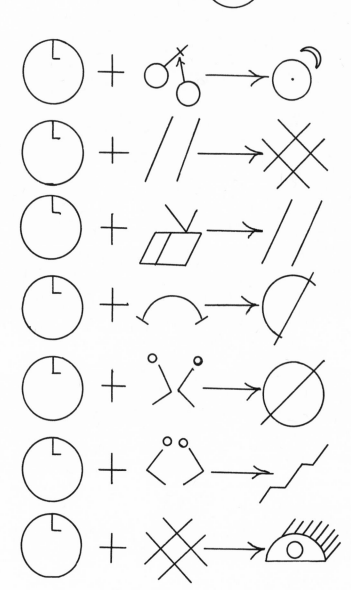

Hate

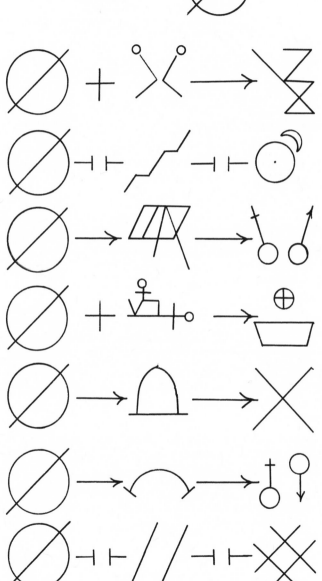

SONG OF LOVE

The characteristics of love depend upon the individuals and the forces current between them. If the forces can be modified, if the current can be magnified then the love becomes transformed into a purer, more magnificent cohesive force.

The nucleus of being consists of a core with other qualities orbiting around it. Qualities such as dishonesty, fear, inefficiency and pain diminish, dampen and decrease the radiations of the core. Qualities such as honesty, trust and pleasure amplify increase and magnify the radiations. Replacing the negators with positive amplifiers transforms the radiations into intense emanations, the vibrations of humanity.

It is the environment surrounding the core that moves love up or down, depressing or elevating it. It is the environment about love that cools or heats it, freezes it or leaves it free flowing and ever expanding.

Rays of warmth sensitizing against pain, rays of multisplendored waves passing through crystals of positivity, become accelerated into surging energies of enveloping love. Changing the swirl about the core from negative to positive changes the outward throb of the core permitting it to oscillate in freedom, expanding with each vibratory movement into an accelerating momentum to joy.

Love is the essential pleasure of life elevating the being. Love is the essence of Life's throb. It's the beat of all desire, the pulse of the universe.

Love washes and cleanses with gentle ways. It purifies with pleasure. It magnifies enriching the body and the mind.

Love refracted through the prisms of negativity diminishes. It becomes neglected, imprisoned and squeezed down. It becomes frozen.

Refracted through the prisms of hurt and fear, love becomes a source of pain instead of pleasure. Hate and frustration contaminate it further. Dishonesty heaps on more dirt. Deflected through the prisms of negativity, love is turned against itself, killing its possessor.

Love encourages every muscle, nerve and cell into a greater efficiency of action. It encourages every action, coordinated movement, harmony and creation. Love is the core of Life. Those who love life must love others and themselves. The lack of love thwarts all biologic existence. When the very center of Life becomes weakened, all energies are scattered, thrown out of phase. The biologic rhythms are forced off tune. Harmony changes to noise. None learning, none effective, beings result doomed to repeat in endless repetition past mistakes.

The negators, the negative modifiers, are infective agents surrounding the core of life, enclosing the intrinsic drives, smothering, strangling and diminishing them. Entering into the intrinsic urges, the negators pollute them and split them apart causing them to spew forth efforts enfeebled and often against life itself. The regulatory mechanisms of the organism are forced out of phase and there results a loss of growth, a loss of maturity, a loss of abilities and perceptions.

The weave of Love is made up of beams of admiration, rays of wonder, streams of generation pulsating forward, on to diversity, on to the plan of varied movement to delight the senses. The fabric gladdens the mind, energizes the heart and fills with the warm glow of joy.

Love is an emotion moving people to people and people to life. It's a motion of happiness. It's a movement of pleasure.

Where an atmosphere of love permeates the environment other

qualities of the core can flourish such as creativity. Mature love broadens choices, immature love narrows them down. The immature are fearful and fear inhibits. Mature love overcomes obstacles, immature love is hindered by them. Love propels the mature forward and holds the immature back. Where an atmosphere of love permeates the environment, inhibitions melt away and people move together.

Love is a way of giving and the way an individual gives determines his abilities to love. To give with hesitation, to give with pain, is to love hesitantly, weakly and with fear. To give generously is to love generously.

Systems mold and the mold that restrains makes poor. Poverty people are people poor in abilities to do, to give, to receive and perceive. They are poor to act, to think and to be. They are poor.

Love is a way of receiving and the way an individual receives determines his abilities to love. Poor receivers, poor perceivers, poverty stricken in awareness are not able to receive many messages of love.

Love is a way of being and the way an individual is determines his abilities to love. A being filled with the negators, filled with pain and fear, filled with dishonesties and lack of imagination, filled with distrust and lack of belief in life is an individual of diminished capabilities to love. Poverty people are poor in abilities. They are poor!

People filled with noise, clanging conflict and complaint, are people who perceive noise. To perceive love, people need to perceive beyond the noise; and as the love comes through, the noise tends to fade away. As the being becomes more in tune with love, awareness widens and he perceives with gladness the vibrations wherever he looks.

The earth and all its beings, every creature, every molecule and atom vibrate with the hum of love. Love is the essential element of life and the earth is full of life and growing fuller.

Systems that coerce the giving cripple the abilities to love.

Systems that coerce the receiving cripple the abilities to love. Systems that provoke fear inhibit the capabilities to love. Systems that evoke dishonesties diminish all.

Love is goodness. It makes life. It adds intensities to existence. It adds a happy tempo moving to joy. Goodness moves to joy and joy moves to goodness. No quality exists in isolation. They all feed into each other intensifying or diminishing.

The song of love is a tune of desire, a tune for goodness and changing, making better, improving, making more efficient, modifying, making more pleasing, evoking pleasure. The song of love is a happy song, warm and crystal clear.

Love is the way for life. Without it life is meaningless. It is purposeless. It is sad, cruel, painful and full of suffering and despair. With love it brightens. Sadness is banished, and life takes on purpose, meaning and color.

Love nourishes life. Life nourishes love. Love and life are so intimately related, so intimately intertwined that the two cannot truly be separated, differentiated or distinguished. Without love there can simply be no life, and infants shrivel up and die right away, and grownups shrivel up and die more slowly.

Without love the greatest biologic creation with the most magnificent potential for creation becomes a frustrated mechanism full of violence and destruction. It becomes a hate filled hurt mechanism crippled in its potential and unable to carry out its function. It turns against itself and destroys.

The core gains strength from nutrition, not the nutrition of food, but of love, not the liquid of water but of imagination, of trust and honesty. The core gains strength from light, the oscillating pulsations of pure energy. The light brightens the core, sets it vibrating in excitement compelling it to motion, the motion of expansion, the movement of life.

Without light there is no exposure. Without learning and stimulation the being shrivels and plunges into darkness. Without variety, differences, the motion slows, becomes less and the glow diminishes.

Love!

       Love!

              Love!

                     Concern for the Future!

Love!

       Love!

              Love!

                     Transcends the limits of self!

Love is a pouring forth of energy in awe and reverence. It's a longing urging to unite, a longing surging in delight, coloring all in splendor. It's a multicolored whirl of brilliance flashing through the mind, brightening the vision. It's a crystal force pure and tender, focusing all beams in magnificent variety and kindness, filling with the desire to give.

Love is life's treasure, a pleasure without measure, a fortune forever growing, throwing out rays of kindness, gentleness and desire. It's caring and concern.

Love needs honesty to make it grow, trust to make it expand and sex to excite the flow. It's softness and the desire to caress. It's pleasure and the promise of more.

Love is electric rays of magnetic current, pulling gently, sweetly and filling with warmth. Love is the essential pleasure of life changing the chemistries of the brain, elevating the perceptions. The secretions of pain are far different from the secretions of pleasure. The pleasure fluids stimulate to perceive more, move more, do more and love more.

Love is a process of unforced development, a process of coherence and organization. Love is a spontaneous development without strain. It is a process strengthened by knowledge and experience, increased by usage.

Our creations are parts of our love. They are parts of ourselves, parts that move beyond our finite flesh of being, sparking vibrations to eternity. Our creations are parts of our actions and our actions should always move with love.

Communication

Noncommunication

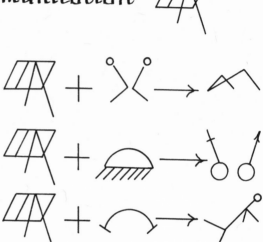

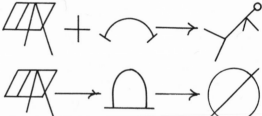

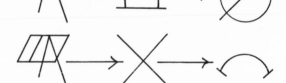

SONG OF COMMUNICATION

There's a hum. There's movement. Electrons spin and interact. There's a hum. It's communication! Electrons spin and interact and molecules grow closer together, mature into a more intimate relationship and the hum becomes stronger. Millions of molecules vibrate together. Billions of molecules begin to sing in a rhythm uniquely their own and then there is a cell.

The song grows stronger. The hum increases. Out of vibrations, oscillations come waves of undulations producing a movement, a coalescence, a coming together in unison. And out of that union the song of harmony creates a new form of being, a form we call life, a form of billions of molecules communicating in a harmony of music, awesome and wonderful to contemplate.

The song grows stronger. Communication binds, holds together, makes for excitement, movement, patterns and life. The song grows stronger and billions of cells begin to coalesce. More intimate patterns of varied vibrations, undulating waves of radiations pour forth and out of this song of being cells unite and form complex organisms. They differentiate into kidney and spleen. They move and change into lung and heart. They vibrate and dance into patterns of skin and bone. They shake and become more sensitive and move into brain and nerves, muscle and intestine. But each cell communicates with the next. Each sings its song and is alert to the singing all about. Each group of cells, groups called organs, communicates with the others, coordinates and the vibrations coalesce into a more intricate, stronger, more capable form of being able to affect, to change, to modify its environment.

51

The hum increases. The hum is life! The hum matures, becomes stronger, able, capable of doing and of being. The hum joins in a symphony of hums, of song, of music full of delight. The hum is energy, movement, constant changing, rotating, oscillating, vibratory movement, energy out of the night. The song is energy, vibrations of electricity shining bright. The song is light! The song is light!

The greater the communication, the more intense becomes the song. The more the articulation, the greater becomes the quality of being. The clearer each note, the sharper and more pure each tone becomes, the more magnificent becomes the music.

The song is for movement and movement is life. The song is energy moving out of collision and out of strife. The song is a love song of beauty and truth. The song is a wave, a wave of youth ever growing, changing, increasingly changing, moving, making, uniting and forming designs so intricate, so lovely and divine.

The song stirs to action, causes reaction, makes for retraction of all confusion and despair. The rhythm is catching, compelling and magnetic, sweeping up to movement, evoking more change. Hear? Hear! Hear the hum.

And the music has words, symbols, too. Listen! Hear the words, the symbols that add meaning to the scheme.

Communication is an adaptation for increasing cooperation, making for abilities exceeding the sum. Communication is information to be used, vibrations capable of being reproduced.

Communication is information capable of being stored, patterns of vibrations moving through time and space, patterns of excitation granted to the human race. It shapes us, makes us the kind of beings we are. It shakes us, breaks us or makes us even more.

Memories passing through time and space, a continuity with each moment past, make us more with each pulse beat. With each tongue beat setting designs in the air, with each pen beat recording the patterns of thought, with each flow of rhythms life moves on.

Experience recorded adds to our store. Glands secrete according to plan. The cardiac muscle has an intrinsic beat. We are formed by information, shaped by a design. We are molded by experience, fired by patterns of thought.

Words are symbols meant to be used. They aid us in controlling, moving, shaping the environment all about. Words are vibrations which we send forth, radiations that shape the conditions all about us, signals that influence, they try to move.

Words are tools to shape the future, brighten the present and give more meaning to the past. Words are a means of expressing vibrations, messages compelling greater adhesion, making more powerful all that is done.

Words form messages and messages give meanings. Information, knowledge increases the perceptions, enlarges the sensations, increases the whole. The messages form designs of categorizing and understanding. They set the course for the infinite vibrations to follow and go.

Minds increase in complexity as radiations pour in. Experience adds to the memory banks. Knowledge adds to the stores. And the greater the patterns, the intricate designs, the greater the recordings, the delicate bits, the more the vital processes expand and grow. Evolution involves new ways for chemical transactions essential to life, assuring more change.

Greater complex organizations permitting a greater influence means an increasing communication between the environment and the self. Communication between individuals growing more intense means an increase of energies. The energies hum.

There's a hum. Electrons flow, rotate and undulate. They form a pattern all their own. Electrons dance and collide, form together, and they grow into a pattern more intricate than before. Atoms form molecules. The electrons spin. Molecules form cells and cells form organs. Organs form individuals and individuals form the earth. The earth is a planet spinning about the sun. The sun is a star moving in a galaxy.

And energy and matter are inter-changeable. Matter forms energy but energy forms matter. Energy is movement and movement is change.

Cells collide and clang, bang into a roar of confusion, a rush of noise. Energies fall wasted, exhausted and spent. Cells collide; motion is changed; spinning is altered as they collide again. Cells suffer as they change overcoming inertia, forced to extend their range. Cells clash and in the clashing reverberate together and communication is established and once established, it grows. Energies fall into alignment. Energies fuse. Noise changes to music and the notes begin to harmonize.

Clear, pure, exact and precise notes add beauty to the whole. Clear, pure, exact, precise messages transmit efficiency to the whole. And the whole is ever greater than the sum of its parts. The whole is ever stronger, more capable of excitement, more meaningful and able to do. As each cell becomes more dependent upon the next communicating stronger in a relationship of fusion, each cell gains in longevity and well being, too.

There's a hum of communication, a hum of love. There's a hum of living motion interacting and setting vibrations aglow.

Each being needs others to give it meaning and glow. Each being needs others to transmit the patterns through time and through space. Each being needs others to add to its light. Each being needs others to fill it with delight.

The messages hum. They thunder. They roar. The notes become purer, the music more divine.

The messages form bridges from past to the present, from present to future, too. They form predictions of movement and patterns, messages to be read. But who has the knowledge, the ability, the skill? Who has the perceptions? Who has the will?

Who has the glow of gladness, the brightness, the light? Who can project his being far through the night? Who can read the vibrations, the signals divine? Who? Who can sing God's praises in tones most pure? Who can transmit his feelings moved by Love? Who can transcend the confusion and find order in it all?

Sing and the song grows strong. Sing and it becomes more clear. Sing of dreams and meanings. Sing of union and of love. Sing and the song grows stronger filling the singer with its might. The song is communication and communication brings together. That's the purpose. That's the plan, increasing intellectual abilities.

Creativity

Destruction

SONG OF CREATION

Creation is a way of building, laying foundations and erecting structures. Creation is an awesome unfolding of a magnificent plan of expansion, ways of improving, recombining and designing beings of beauty and goodness and elegant objects too.

Creation is an efficient use of energies for goodness, pleasure and joy, the joy of movement, and evolving into more each day. Creation is an exchange, a merging of patterns into something new.

Creation is a striving, a moving forward to something better, correcting, improving and making more. It's an inter-relationship of love and imagination, of honesty and efficiency, of a desire to leave a mark in the holy scheme. Creation started as a dream, vibrated and radiated and became a scheme that unfolded, developed and expanded and expands still to infinity.

Creation is the direction, the purpose, the means for obtaining joy. It's the interaction, the attraction that propels forward. It's the discovery, the adventure, the recombination, the thrill of variety, and it's more.

It's the thirst for knowledge, the brain waves growing in glowing intensities and able to direct the body into motions more accurate, movements more exact patterns of beauty to please the soul. Creation banishes pain, banishes sorrow, eliminates loneliness as it gives identity. It brings questions, answers, still more questions, still more answers—concentric cycles of energy always moving out.

What identity? The identity of man. What is man? Coherent

energy, a part of God, different from other energies, it's true. Man is capable of more creation, more imagination, more of the powers to do. Man is God's finest creation upon the earth but he must forever unfold. Man evolves and God does, too. God is dynamic, ever moving and the laws of the universe always involve motion.

To help in creation, we must create. To be part of creation, we must create, create ourselves into better beings, create the earth into a more harmonious place.

On the level of base emotion, creativity is hindered and often turns to destruction. But as the emotional level moves up, so does the pulse of being and creativity becomes more pure. The emotions move the being, setting motions into being. Hormones secrete and compel reaction. Messages fly and there's interaction of heart and brain, of blood and chemistries and nerves, of hormones and of glands.

Creativity in joy moves the flow in a synchronized harmonious glow. The impulses of heart and brain fling their coordinated energies stronger. Life increases, becomes longer and more active, too.

No cell can exist alone, no cell can be lonely in the wondrous plan making up the scheme of man. And in the design of humanity, no individual can truly be free unless he interacts and recharges his energies with others. To be alone is to run down. It's counter to creativity.

Man is light of multichanneled flow. Man is light of a multichanneled glow. He needs and craves variety. Variety is an element of creation to join imagination in the fine weave mixed with truth, mixed with efficiency and forming life.

The patterns of thought change the electrical waves of the brain and the patterns of electromagnetic cerebral energy change the energies of the body, changing structure and changing function, changing function feeding back to structure. Cycles, concentric circles of power, are set into being and the being grows ever more. It's a self perpetuating plan set up to the perfection of man according to the Creator whose intelligence supreme is beyond the imagination of the most mystic dream struggling to fire the flame and move to eternity.

Creation requires love, requires communication, requires all the intricate strands, the rays, the beams of the internal light. And it requires more. It demands the concentration of the circling modifiers to make it cohesive and strong.

Gasping grasps of revelation come only with the lightening flashes of honesty, shining the way to creation. The revelation makes for visions, dreams of days yet to be born in brightness and full of life.

The flashes of truth hum and vibrate, growing in glowing intensities until no longer flashes but steady beams, truth reveals what the vision can see. Under this light is creation formed. Under this light do we grow to understand that the greatest freedom yet to be is the freedom of spontaneous inter-action, the joy of exchange. The greatest of all creation is intimate communication, a teaching and learning, too, the joy of giving and receiving, the joy of being and becoming.

Creation needs sweetness. It needs spice. It requires all the threads of life to warm it and make it glow, make it move on evermore. The joy of giving and receiving, the joy of being and becoming, that's creation.

Creation excites! It stimulates the soul into a higher plane of conscious awareness, increasing receptivity, increasing the cerebral message flow, magnifying the signals for Life, multiplying the sparks into a stream, moving on to the dream of union, forming radiation beams of communion.

From the waters to the land, from the land to the skies, from the sky out to space, ever moving, the human race extends its efforts outward. Outward go inventions moving man further. Outward goes communication moving man closer. Outward rolls knowledge increasing man's awareness. Outward go the vehicles moving man beyond the earth to the birth of days born in joy and freedom.

The greatest freedom yet to be is the freedom of reactivity, interactions and exchange, reactions that increase the range. Humanity moves beyond this world. The plan becomes unfurled. Sparks become a stream, the stream dances into beams and focuses on the stars. Humanity moves out.

Mortality

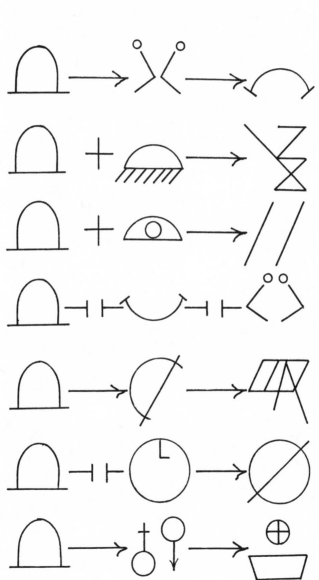

Immortality ☽◉

SONG OF IMMORTALITY

Send the being out, out through the night. Let the spark float past all the body's restraint. Catch a glimmer now and then from the past. Use the glimmer for the fuel to let the soul float free.

Feel the compulsion that pulls, the magnetic rays that compel. Feel the force for union pushing you on as well. Feel the urgings stirring. Let the soul float free towards the mystery of being.

Beyond the darkness, the turmoil and despair, beyond the sensation honed by pain; beyond the darkness is the light, the brilliant, awesome, magnificent light.

Beyond all time and all space is the forward thrust of energy, vibrant, vital, verve. The soul floats free. Free to expand, free to serve, free to answer, one big nerve for receiving energy. The soul floats free.

Motion, motion, accelerating motion, heightened, inspired, fired by life. Movement, movement, purposeful movement, moving according to a patient plan. Rotating, vibrating, orderly movement resulting from the scheme of things.

Fire the soul with questions. Fire the soul with love. Fire it with imagination. Speed it on its way.

Question! Question! Question! What is the soul? A spark of life! A spark of life? Electric energy able to move. Magnetic energy able to compel. Useful energy able to do. Communicating energy charging and changing to something new.

Energy! Vibrant waves cascading into torrents of magnetic flames casting vibrations all about. Energy! The soul is energy, energy that grows, that uses vehicles in order to move. Energy moving in pulsating throbs, casting off light as it moves on its way, gaining substance, sustenance from other souls, ordered patterns of magnificent growth.

The soul floats free, humming energy forever growing more, energy to move bodies, pure energy and nothing more. Prime mover of the biologic machine, the soul expands according to use. Use the soul and the soul expands, abuse the soul and it retracts from the body leaving it cold, cold and old and dying, too.

In the flight for union, there's a design of intricate movement of color and dance. Rolling energy gaining momentum as it gains in powers of direction over chance. Moving energy pouring in laughter towards its source. The soul expands.

What is matter? What is life? What is laughter? What is strife? What is the body? What is the soul? What is God and immortality?

Fire the soul with questions. Fire it with knowledge, too. Fire the soul with open memory patterns, open ways to perceive. Open! Open! Let the soul free.

Matter and energy are interchangeable. Crystallized energy forming a pattern of coordinated information, set to a rhythm, a symphony of being and of growth. The infant is conceived and it unfolds according to a preordained plan, an open plan, open to infinite modifications, open to man.

The world must be free, free to act and interact. Free to fly to eternity. Free to question! Free! Free! Free to expand in energy.

What is death? Who can answer? Ask again! What is death? Feel the chill of clutching fear. Is it the end of all being? Is it the end of all seeing? Is it the end of all giving? The end of all receiving? Is it the end? The end?

The soul forever expands. It moves on according to a preordained plan open to infinite modifications, open to infinite ways of being, ways of flight, ways of acceleration, ways of light, ways of darkness, or ways of might.

Death! Death is the change in a form of matter bringing about a disorder in a pre-established plan. Electricity ceases to function.

Communication stops. Energy radically diminishes and eventually ceases to be.

The soul is energy, expanding energy. It fires the body. It sparks the way. The soul is part of all eternal light. Can the soul cease to be?

Fire the soul with questions. Let the thoughts float free.

The soul is open to modification, forever open to change. It uses the body as a vehicle from which to extend its range. Bodies die, souls expand. Bodies are vehicles. Souls are energies, pure energies. Bodies are organized, intricate, coordinated bits of information, patterns of movement, of signals forming unique patterns. Bodies are trillions upon trillions of repetitive yet changing bits of information continuously being communicated. Bodies die when the information stops being communicated but what about the soul?

Fire the soul with questions. Accelerate its flight! All the same but different. Repetitive patterns ever changing, those are memory stores. Electrical waves exchanging and mutually charging, those are waves of thought. Happy thoughts beat out a fast rhythm, an orderly open scheme. Unhappy waves are slow and disordered, not coordinated or clear.

Speed up the rhythm. Find order in the scheme. What are we really? What if it's all a dream? What are dreams really? Patterns of electrical discharge?

Question! Question! Fire the questions. Try to answer. Modify the answer. Open! Open! Forever open. Open up the thoughts. It's all the same yet different and the differences excite. All of knowledge has union but the patterns are all unique.

The body can fall to disorder but never the beating soul. The soul is pure energy, pulsating, unfolding energy using a biologic system for expression, for interaction, for union and knowledge, too.

Fire the soul with pleasure. Increase the tempo a bit. Give it open, pleasing answers, honest answers open to modification, yet part of an expanding scheme. Fire the soul with sunshine, action and happy dreams.

Rolling, unfolding energy! Energy! Energy! And what is energy? Pause and gasp. Turn for information. Never ignore. Always ask more. No restrictions!! The soul must expand!

In the beginning there was darkness and then came the light. Ah! And what is light? Theories! Stepping stones for acquiring knowledge. And with each change of knowledge new patterns of matter appear.

Light and energy, energy and matter; there are relationships we know, relationships that unfold with knowledge, organized orderly patterns for coordinating information, open orderly patterns. Patterns, patterns ever changing moving at accelerating rates. Open up the being. Let the soul throb to the Universal beat. Have trust in the Creator. He's kinder than you. Similar? Yes. It's all interrelated. And what is God?

God is the universe unfolding, all the energy throughout it all. God is the sum total of all being, the sparking master pattern to it all. God is the energy and the light, the originator always moving into unique and pleasing ways.

God is the earth and all the sunshine, the animals and all the stars. God is all the energy that moves. God is the sum total of it all, all unfolding, growing, moving. God is the original spark to the happy scheme.

Open up the being. Strive forever to be. Follow the urges. They lead to immortality.

When the seven lights form and fuse into the holy being of the soul, they inter-relate in such intimate form that they are difficult to differentiate. They are similar yet different too and the differences excite.

Every statement about each light may seem like repetition and yet each statement is different, too, and the differences excite.

The differences lead to knowledge and expand each and every light, each and every of the holy seven strands, and as the fibers interweave they exchange sparks for growth and the soul throbs forward. The soul expands with open perception through receptions growing ever more.

Seven strings of being form the inner light, the core of that which makes us all unique. And about our inner sun rotate the paired modifiers, each one inter-relating and interpenetrating and effecting our soul

Once in a while there's a flash and with my imagination I catch a glimmer, a vision of what is yet to be. I gasp in awe, in wonder and in joy.

Beyond the structured perceptions of mankind, beyond the struggle and the strain, honed by the crystals of honesty are the mystic perceptions of all being. I gasp in awe, in wonder and in joy. I am saddened by what I am but gladdened by what will be.

Floods of inspiration fill my being and vibrate out to eternity. And a mystic vision of happiness stands revealed for fetal humanity yet to be born.

Trust

Fear

SONG OF TRUST

Trust is having faith. It's believing. It's tied up with love and honesty. It's the opposite of fear.

Trust is warmth. It's relaxed muscles and blood vessels. It's a free flow of current pouring forth, moving out for communication, moving for a coming together, moving out into oscillations reverberating in harmony.

To trust is to open up the circuits of humanity, the widening electric circles of life. To trust is to have happy expectations, to regard the immediate future cheerfully. It is the expectation that communications will be accurately received, perceived and returned.

To trust is to have confidence, to open up the mind and the heart in unimpeded movement, in a decisiveness of action. Our sensory organs fire back information to the brain and to act upon that information to the brain is to trust it, to have faith in its accuracy. To approve of another's transmission of perceptions, to approve of another's abilities to communicate without distortion, is to trust.

Trust at its most primitive level requires unqualified faith. Trust on a mature level requires understanding, insight, an ability to perceive with accuracy, clarity and efficiency. It requires honesty.

Bright, clear, clean vision enables trust to function most efficiently. No vision clouded by fear or anger or hatred can allow mature trust to exist. No depressed views of man or life, no degrading habits abusing life, no demeaning actions scornful of the potential of life can permit the exercise of a mature, evolving, increasing, growing, powerful force of trust.

To trust maturely is to have an open faith in one's own perceptions, a faith confirmed by experience, a faith brightened by one's opinion of his fellow men.

The immature are hurt when their trust is unconf rmed, or proven wrong. The mature attempt to learn from their experience in strengthening their powers of perception. The immature are continually weakened. The mature are continually strengthened.

Trust must work in open circuits, circuits for obtaining and utilizing information, circuits for increasing awareness and learning. Trust in closed circuits becomes corrupted by fear and pain. In an open system, it expands and joins in vibrant harmony all the forces for goodness moving man.

Actions contrary to the core of man are actions not to be trusted. And if one cannot trust his own actions, he has lost his power to control his own being. He becomes a creature of mere habit, an automaton reacting in past patterns, spinning down to oblivion.

Mature trust reinforces a faith in life, a belief system consonant with the pulsating forces of the Universe. It does not disregard information, repress or reject information. It correlates and learns. No barriers to information flow are tolerated.

Closed systems tend to stimulate fears, make for distrust and reduce perceptions. Closed systems make for dishonesty, run counter to trust and impede the flow of life. They strangle trust.

Trust accepts diversity excited by new patterns, by varied stimuli of thought and being. It reduces barriers to all sorts of communication accepting data in a well coordinated expansive system of learning.

Trust is a force of cohesiveness, of identification free from anxiety, unburdened by unhappy thoughts. It's a force for identity, identity with humanity, with the forces of the universe, with the life force itself.

The repercussions of trust sound notes of infinite richness. They sound honesty, efficiency, identity. They sound imagination and pleasure.

Trust is a pleasure giving force encouraging investigation.

Hearts beat stronger. The biologic rhythms increase in intensity. The perfusion of messages and blood flow increases. The entire organism, body and mind, turns on with trust as infinite currents gather strength, vibrate together and pour out.

As the powers of trust grow, so do the powers of discrimination. Information is recognized from misinformation by its arhythmic tendencies to fit into the scheme, the scheme of life, the modifying force for growth and evolution. Information is differentiated from misinformation by knowledge, experience, an open minded, open current doubting. Misinformation is discerned by its patterns, its tendencies to set up barriers and hinder the movement, the outward going movement of person to person and individual to life.

Misconceptions go with fear, with angry frustrations and hatred, too. Misconceptions go with inabilities and harmful self images. They go with inarticulated feeling blocking communication. They don't go with trust.

Trust is a cleansing, clearing, crystalizing force. It's a color filled force full of varied motion. It's a force for devotion to the powers of life.

With distrust there is a shift of blood flow. Fear changes the distribution of blood to the intestinal tract and blood pressure rises. The heart rate increases. Adrenaline pours. Blood vessels constrict. There's a relative lack of oxygen in some tissues. The metabolic rate increases. Metabolic acids accumulate. Fear demands fight or flight. It's a force splintering away. It's a force for competition not for coordinated sustained cooperation. It's a splintering force frightening away. It alters the neurochemistry of the brain and narrows the vision.

Fear filled people cannot be trusting. They have an inability to accept situations in a different setting or context. They are hobbled in their efforts to lead useful lives. They are filled with unnecessary cruelties and arbitrary handicaps.

Fear depresses, trust excites. Fear causes aversions, trust attracts. Fear runs contrary to trust in every way.

Systems provoking fear are systems that hinder trust. They are systems counter to life, counter to a richness and variety in being, counter to experience and learning, counter to movement and growth. Fear smothers the essence of humanity.

The hum of life is movement. Increased movement changes a hum to a note. The note of trust releases positive forces that add and amplify.

Variety causes cross fertilization. Trust makes welcome variety in all its infinite forms. It excites to exploration, it fires the imagination to penetrate and to learn. Senses become primed for receptivity. The most delicate of vibrations become able to be perceived. Sensitivities develop leading to increased pleasures, greater joys.

Trust is an essential element for the spirit to use. Without it there can be no expansion. Without it the flavor of life is flat.

Trust is an energizer filling full of power, moving to do. It's essential for all creative motivation. It's necessary for all spontaneous motion.

Strong people have trust in their abilities. They have trust in being able to cope with their environment. They have trust in the future, in their creations and they have trust in the force for life. Trust sweeps the soul forward with light filled dreams.

Pleasure

Pain

SONG OF PLEASURE

Soft, gentle, warm is pleasure. Envigorating, soothing, attracting is pleasure. Pleasure is the Life Force moving to joy. Pleasure is a feeling of contentment, a feeling of happiness, an emotion compelling expression.

Pleasure is a sweet urge for sharing. It's a feeling of well being. It's a surge of gay feelings lifting the being into increased awareness. Colors become more intense. Receptors become primed, more easily reactive, more easily stimulated and moved.

Pleasure moves out to other beings. The patterns of neural discharges change in rhythm and intensities. The patterns of hormonal secretions change, too. The very chemistries of the body become subtly altered changing the perceptions all about.

Pleasure heals and healing moves further. It urges to improvement, to accomplishment, to doing. Knowledge obtained through pleasure is knowledge happily retained. That which is learned through pleasure is always remembered. That learned through pain, we try to forget.

Pleasure is the opposite of pain, an expansive force for goodness, a happy power for beauty. Pleasure is the emotion that excites to life sending the sparks flying, igniting the flames of being into a fire of dancing energies moving on to ecstasy, swinging up to God.

Pleasure elates. It brightens. It heightens and it awes. Pleasure delights. It moves to union. It makes for Life. Pleasure is totally the opposite of pain.

Pain narrows, the perceptions shut down. Pain causes retractions. It inhibits action, diminishes vision and decreases motion all around. The motion of pain is a motion of withdrawal, spastic motion jerky and arhythmic. Pain provokes to anger, hatred and fear. It makes for destruction. Pain pollutes pleasure making it less clear, less intense and less exhilarating.

Pain provokes the negators into action. It provokes dishonesty, inefficiency and distrust. The motion of pain is contrary to pleasure.

Pain protects only by repelling. Pleasure enhances only by attracting. Pleasure attracts to Life and gives Life meaning. But the pleasures of maturity differ from the pleasures of childhood. The pleasures of purity differ from the pleasure of pollution.

Immature pleasures center about the point of self. Immature pleasure concerns primarily the receiving. Mature pleasures move in wider fields and concern primarily the giving. The warm waves of mature pleasure move out and its reverberations fill with strong and joyous vibrations.

Polluted pleasures, contaminated with pain, are pleasures deflected, weakened waves echoing untrue, off key, and unclear. The reverberations are often too weak to hear or feel. Polluted pleasures are puny, setting up only faint vibrations, shadows of what should be.

Any system that so weakens the emotion of joy, any system that so confuses the forces of pleasure and pain, and any system that so decreases the being, is a system that casts down from the very movement of life. Life is movement up and out. Evolvement is the purpose of being and systems that decrease the forces of evolution are systems against the purpose of Life.

Pleasure triggers movement into realms of music vibrant with color, into attitudes of freedom and expansion. Limits expand. Feedback becomes increased and with it comes increasing self correction. Reactions become more carefully monitored and brought under greater thinking control. Increasing self correction makes for strength. It involves increasing feedback, the gathering and understanding of more and more bits of information. It involves an increasing perception of relationships.

The thoughts set waves of electricity vibrating through the brain, waves which wash through the body influencing function and structure as well. Increasing self correction leads to more efficient function, to more beautiful structure and to a greater ability to do.

Slow output follows pain. Rapid output follows pleasure. Pleasure makes for high movement individuals accelerating as they go.

Man is a creature who must always alter his environment. Pleasure makes man most capable of accomplishing this end. The cycles set into motion are open cycles in contrast to the cycles of pain.

The receptor requirements for fine vibratory perception are demanding. Within each receptor all communication must be accurate, exact, and clear. There can be no conflict in messages, no hesitation or obscure reaction. The light source must be strong.

As interest in the environment increases, more information is obtained. With this increase comes a flow of cerebral messages, stores of memories are put away ready to trigger a multi-pattern complex flow.

Enlarging the data gathering thought organizations bring about a greater ability to be stimulated. The finer the receptors, the more capable they are of response.

Pleasure enhances perception. Pain shuts it down. Pleasure enhances abilities to make choices. It makes for flexibility.

Pleasure encourages and increases the capabilities to gather knowledge and makes that knowledge and experience more readily available for use. The normal heart is controlled through nervous and humoral channels that are responsive to a variety of body actions and functions. Pleasure encourages feedback to the heart and from the heart to the brain. The channels hum and with the hum, life becomes more vibrant.

Pain diverts the being's energies into channels oriented solely about the self. Pleasure expands the energies into enlarging fields. Pain prevents perceptions due to the din of internal alarms obscuring and distorting. Pleasure enhances perception increasing the interest, widening the field, expanding the awareness into a greater yield of feedback and abilities, too.

The radiations from the self are intensified by pleasure. The self opens up and quickens its movement out as it finds pleasure, warmth, and enjoyment. The self finds purpose in pleasure and pleasure in purpose. It is moved by creation, and the entire life style quickens as the self steps out to pleasure.

The degrees of pleasure an individual is able to find structures his relationship towards others. The entire social structure becomes modified permitting a greater degree of interactions and cross stimulations. Pleasure increases reactivity. It increases reactions.

A mere trace of pain in pleasure markedly decreases the speed of reaction, the sense of enjoyment, the motion of joy. A mere trace of pain is often enough to obscure meanings. It diminishes the abilities to grasp relationships and thereby decreases awareness and understanding.

Pleasure is the catalyst to all motion, the prompter of movement, the thrill to life's very beat. It brightens the present and the future and illuminates the past.

The waters of life are stirred by pleasure setting up waves of energy vibrating to the very core of being. Puny pleasures make puny ripples. Little pleasures make little swells. Thunderous pleasures creates walls of massive oscillations, living energies tuned to life.

Pleasure caresses soft and gentle. It soothes and washes away all fury, shining up the face of truth. It clears the vision, helps define what life may do, and deepens the elastic channels in which life may run.

Pure pleasure is crystalline. It speeds life processes, quickening, strengthening, coloring the steps.

Pleasure speeds internal development. It accelerates the growth of maturity increasing the fluid flow of information, synchronizing and harmonizing the current into efficient streams.

Hence, society which attempts to produce conditioned aversions to pleasure sets up internal conflicts, contradictions and competitions. The result is often an individual frozen to his natural urgings, finding movement ever painful.

Past nutrition influences present appetites. Past pleasure determines present capabilities and desires. Pleasure poor people can respond to little pleasures. Pleasure rich people respond to rich pleasures.

Pleasure must start from within. Then as it grows it comes from without and from within. The environment encourages the growth. Then the pleasure increases and in the growing gains in force. The force within radiates out, glowing, brightening, and charging the environment without, enlarging its confines, transforming the quality of lives.

Those afflicted with pains are under pressure, diverting energies merely for repair. They are under strain to confine the affliction. They are in turmoil full of raucous fury. The pain provokes other negators throwing out bonds of intermingling restraints, a complex network to obscure and confine the inner light.

These people feel submerged and lost. Their past is pain, Pain repels. Hence, they flee from the past. Their present is painful and their future clouded with the present. They feel cornered, trapped, caught in a squeeze. They are under tension, under pressure, under stress, undermining their images, forcing them into actions against their well being. They are in a closed circle of distress, unwitting killers of themselves.

Pleasure coordinates and concentrates brain power. It is the primary stimulator of change, a humanizing power unafraid of scrutiny unless contaminated with pain.

Pain is an ache, a void, a feeling depressing, degrading and full of despair. Pain is loneliness and isolation, a feeling of being cut off, alienated and all alone. It fragments the being.

Pain is the ache of desire unfulfilled. It's the ache of failure, the lack of being. Pain is cold, biting, bitter, burning cold, freezing cold, arresting motion, halting thought, stopping being.

Sadness and suffering come with pain. Depression and dullness follow it, too. Downward orientation forces its way.

The body slumps, shoulders hump. The eyes look down. Chin falls on chest. Reactions slow down. Reflexes diminish. All the body processes slow and with the slowing pain pierces more. It cuts! It tears! It turns from life! Every nerve, bone and muscle aches for relief.

Even the movement of the breath slows down. Pain constricts! Pain restricts! Pain confines! It jails! And in the imprisoning, pain pierces deeper, destroying the holy light from above. It fragments the being.

The abilities to perceive are diminished. The flow of messages are decreased. The nerves are weakened. The entire being is filled with stress and tension. The beat of the heart is detensified. It fragments the being.

Pain is the very opposite of pleasure and just as pain casts down and cuts off, so pleasure elevates and makes for union. So pleasure makes whole.

Pain is a feeling of illness searing the Life within, cutting into the cells spewing their contents out in disorder. Pain is chaos, conflict and contradictions causing malfunction. Pain is a misfiring of the fluid flow. It pulsates with violence. It infests with terror, exploded electricity, the fragmentation of life.

Trapped and cheated by the Rat Race? Find it empty, meaningless, futile? Filled with inner discontentment? Want to live for others?

Changes trigger electrical energy which result in more excited states of being. Changes stimulate the rhythmic flow of hormones which increase the output of the heart, increasing the uptake of oxygen from the blood. Energy becomes greater and more efficiently utilized. The beams of being then cover a wider area for experience and information. We suffer deficiency diseases making for less humanity, less movement, less flexibility, less variety and color, making for less life. As the deficiencies decrease, inventiveness increases. Contacts increase.

Increasing contact, movement, interaction, intimacy and learning. Increasing coordination of information and skills combined with increasing flexibility, inventiveness and excitement. Increasing and more maturing cooperation of every degree.

Knowledge increases the potential for stimulation and response. Knowledge increases with experience and information received. A cycle of growth is initiated with electric feedback.

Pain causes antidromic action potentials colliding with the intrinsic currents of being, masking natural flow and confusing the signals to the brain. Pain causes alarm, reactions, constrictions of blood vessels, reduction in the flow of nutriments to the cells which if prolonged results in cellular pathology and eventually death. Pain disrupts the process of learning, the potential for excitation, the consciousness of being, moving, shifting, the cyclic patterns of brain activity into more constricted circles reducing the activated physiologic patterns of movement of the body and brain, reducing the satisfaction of needs associated with intimate involvement with nature and people, an interaction with living at its purest and best, forming a collage of unique adventure for each individual.

Humans respond psychologically and physiologically to their stimulus environment. They and their environment are functionally inseparable.

Annoyances and pain cause detrimental emotional reactions affecting every system of the body. Through its activating effect upon the subcortical neural systems of the brain, unconscious and conscious pain, pain suppressed or admitted, either continuous or intermittent, modifies the pacing by the brain of cardiovascular, endocrine, metabolic, reproductive, and neurological function. Since activating neural systems are themselves restrained by inhibitory neural systems with which they interact and which are also provoked by pain, the reactivity of the organism as a whole is modulated temporally and chronically, according to its own unique past history of pain.

With repeated exposure to irritation, the organism may "learn" both behaviorally and physiologically to partly "ignore," "tune out," and "turn off," hence, reduce the intensity of its perceptions. This doesn't mean that it doesn't respond, or that the response it does make is unimportant. With different chronic levels of irritation, pain, discomfort, different degrees of influences are exerted by the brain upon the peripheral physiological functions and different levels of basal function are maintained. The most profound physiological effects are produced when individuals accustomed to low levels of irritation are startled by an unexpected source of discomfort. Since in many physiological systems, disturbances are dampened only very gradually, the physiological effect of startle may persist for a considerable period of time after the startling event occurs.

While stimulation is necessary for the development of the brain and for the development of every physiological system in the body, irritation is harmful. We are only now beginning to understand the relationship between behavioral and physiologic functions and the stimulus environment.

Pain effects the perceptive mechanisms. But the impairment of perception is but one of the important effects of the environment. There are innumerable effects. There's an interference with speech communication, a hearing loss, an interference with mental work and skill, an impairment of sleep.

Pain impairs perceptions. It also impairs response. There's an interference not only with hearing, feeling, seeing, touching and smelling, but also with speech communication and abilities of expression. There's an interference with mental work and skill and even an impairment of sleep. All power production within the organism is reduced whereas pleasure expands the power production. Pleasure swings the cycles of electricity out. Pain pushes them in.

The addition of toxic substances within the environment causes irritant chemicals to be added to the internal composition.

Alienation

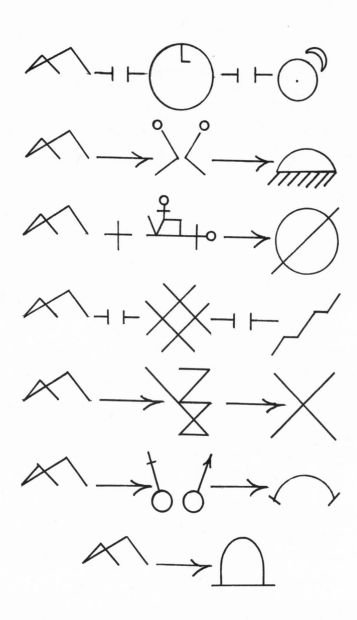

Identity

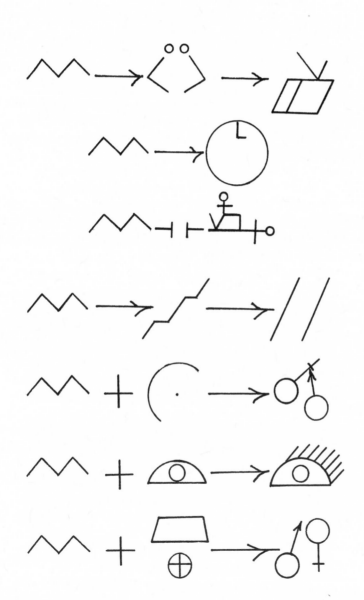

SONG OF IDENTITY

The baby is born. It cries and dimly perceives that through this rudimentary form of communication its needs are met. The baby is born and dimly identifies mother with itself. It is a part of mother and mother appears to be a motor part of itself, an effector organ carrying out its wishes and functioning to supply its needs.

The child grows and begins to develop a superior sensory mechanism. Eye sight improves. It notices other people about, people who also appear to respond to its cries and its smiles. It's picked up by them. Its needs are often also supplied by them. Those others may be siblings, father, aunts, uncles or grandparents. The child broadens its field of identity. It is the center of its own universe, but the concentric circles revolving about the point of self begin to spread out. Like a pebble dropped into still waters the ripples spread out ever expanding circles of identity. The environment expands as its perceptions increase. With growth of its abilities to move and to do the environment expands further.

The child identifies with its room. It grows. It identifies with its house. It grows. It identifies with the area about the house, the neighborhood, the town, the state.

The child's nervous system becomes more exact, more able to discern and discriminate, more efficient and effective. The child identifies with its family and friends, its neighbors, its city people. It identifies with its nation.

With each increase of awareness there is an increase of identification. Awareness tends to flow, expand and increase naturally. Awareness becomes impeded only with negativities. Some negativities are intrinsic. The child is born with fears, fears that must be soothed and quieted if the perceptions are to grow. Other fears are provoked by the environment, a fragmented environment that stresses differences. An environment that is hostile, non-giving and competitive.

The immature organism cannot be stimulated by differences. In its growth it must focus on similarities. Similarities attract it, make it feel safe. Similarities help it to identify.

Differences frighten the immature. They feel threatened. Differences are foreign and the immature tend to reject what they don't understand, don't know, or can not feel as familiar.

Where awareness is arrested, identification is impeded. Fear halts identification. Thoughts stressing differences stop the process of identity for the developing crude organism. Frustration, hatred, anger, cut off the flow.

Wherever curiosity is impeded the waves of identity are impeded. Wherever the negators work, identity often fails. And with the failure of identity comes a failure in awareness, a failure to move forward and to expand in being.

Thoughts which close perceptions, thoughts that hinder perceptions must hinder awareness and must hinder identity. Thoughts which turn to symbols instead of people must hinder identity and awareness. Thoughts which turn from life and joy must hinder awareness and identity. They narrow the vision and turn to pain. Pain arrests and deflects. Pain puts barriers in the way of the concentric circles of awareness making them misshapen. Awareness tries to expand but with pain involved, awareness becomes spotty. Identity becomes distorted.

Identity can only evolve with life. Only with life can identity move forward. Only with the forward pulsation of the heart can identity grow. To be turned from life, to be attuned to symbols instead of meaning, to worship form instead of content, to be competitive instead of cooperative, is to shatter the process of identification.

With splintered identity comes fragmented vision. With fragmented vision comes an unclear awareness, a decreased consciousness, a perversion in the ever expanding moving process of life.

Children like toys. Their imaginations enable them to identify toys with reality. A box represents a building. Another box becomes a car. As they play the symbols take on meanings which hold only for the game. An adult or even a child who persists in thinking that the box is a building has departed from the process of awareness. His consciousness is distorted and his perceptions untrue. The adult who persists in holding symbols more important than life is an adult engaged in a game shutting off his identity with life, closing down his perceptions, filling him with dissentions, with forces against himself.

As awareness expands, identity follows. With increasing identity comes a greater intimacy with all being. There's a merging of being with humanity, a merging with nature, a union with the earth, a communion with the universe. With increasing identity, the consciousness soars into realms of joy, a mystic joy of being.

The inner light glows more intensely. It brightens and illuminates. The vision broadens, ever broadens, evolving in waves of energy, the happy movement of adventure, the excitement of joy.

To fail to identify is to fail in evolvement, to fail in being. To fail to identify is to be alienated, to be filled with coldness, loneliness, isolation and pain. To be alienated is to be a being cut off from purpose, with concentric circles of awareness moving closer, narrower, regressing to the point.

To be alienated is to perceive an environment foreign to the self, an environment greater than the self. The environment seems threatening, beyond the abilities to cope.

Alienated people are people torn with pain, shattered with competition, ripped with confusions. Alienated people are people infected with hatred, anger and frustrations, the symptoms of weakness. They are people cutting off the very force of life.

Unhappy thoughts make for unhappy perceptions. They spew forth the weakness they feel. They vomit out their turmoils, their sadness, their terrible sense of desperation. Life seems beyond them. Death looms ahead.

Reality is that which is in harmony with life, not with games of pretense, fictions of being, artificial ways contrary to nature, contrary to life. Reality is that which is in harmony with increasing awareness, a nervous system growing with energy, expanding its capacities to perceive and to excite. Alienation snuffs out the light.

The child grows and as it grows it must be encouraged with gentle forces, powers of love and praise, happy images about itself and others, tender urgings of the imagination to move out. Alienation counters this growth. Alienation comes from coercion, an environment that tried to bend and break, an environment breaking the spirit, shattering the light within. To be alienated is to become turned from purposeful thought and action, to have dull vision and much pain.

To be alienated is to be filled with an excruciating hunger and too confused to satisfy its urge. Food can't fill it. Toys can't. Houses, clothes, television sets, boats, all the gadgets on earth are useless. The pain, the gnawing hunger tearing inside persists and gets bigger. Duller, dimmer, drearier draws the vision. Unhappier become the thoughts. Weaker becomes the being. Death is welcomed as an end, a solution to the problem, a cessation to the pain.

Alienated people are people at war within themselves. Their weakness spills over. They conflict with others, too. They war, kill, make still. They try and die, doomed to failure by the failure within.

The process of identification is a process of strength, a process of maturity following the laws of nature. And the laws of nature are always laws concerning motion while the laws of coercion are laws of restraint. The process of identification is a movement in harmony with the core, the life forces revolving about love. It's a movement upwards to a better, more beautiful being. It's an unfolding of a poem in honor of life.

Identification makes for tenderness, an increasing delicacy of feeling, a graciousness of humanity compatible with the beauty of the universe. The turns of mature identity are turns for the better. The circles of identity always should move out. They move out most easily when fired by truth. Dishonesty inhibits and halts them. Honesty speeds them.

The murkey gloom of alienation spends its fury with the other negators such as dishonesty, fear, and pain. It helps obstruct the light of the core diminishing its energies, turning the being to useless expenditures of effort and postures.

Identity merges the being with others, surges the soul outward as it moves ever forward on to God. Identity is a necessary tie of being.

Honesty

Dishonesty

SONG OF HONESTY

Every question forces an answer but every question also reveals. That's the key to honesty.

Every question reveals a problem. Every question demands an answer. Every problem demands a solution. And a light has been cast.

Honesty is a crystal amplifying the light of the core. It's an exposure accelerating movement and more. Honesty is fertility, the ability of the brain to register unimpaired perceptions coming through the waves of space. It's registered information readily available, unencumbered by any blocks of the human race.

Honesty is an openness to stimulation, a vitality of expression unmarred by restraint or coercion, unpolluted by pain. It's a full power forcefully exerted, nothing skirted, a capacity for doing work.

Honesty washes clean, clears the vision, makes possible all creation, gives life its color, adds zest to schemes. It asks questions, forces answers. Fires the soul to more noble dreams.

Every question has an answer, every problem a solution, too.

Honesty amplifies, magnifies, enlarges the holy light. It makes for power of self control, enabling meaningful action, actions for improvement's sake. It exerts an influence for power, a power for more life, accurate feedback, free from strife.

It's the essential ingredient for maturity enabling the brain to sustain the integrity of the living organism through the current of information unobstructed and clear. Meaning is acquired through learning, through correlations enabling the neuro-sensory mechanisms to perceive and understand. Honesty sends a helping hand increasing the flow of messages, the waves of communication enabling all creation to evolve into patterns new and more clear, into designs more intricate, into ways more full of joy.

Awareness is awakened. Awareness is expanded. Consciousness grows greater, reflected through the prisms of honesty. Rainbows of thrilling colors appear before the visions gazing through the lenses of honesty.

Ask a single question. Disturb a single concept. Respond to the urges. That's the way of honesty.

Repression, suppression, sublimation, and denial are not the ways of honesty. Honesty is freedom, pure power, ever revealing, never concealing, pointing out the way to greater expansion, the way to intensify living, the way to God.

Honesty is usage urging development to greater joy. It's an action of the mind stimulating function, stimulating reaction to new and varied bits of information, to vibrations it modifies. No deception, no devious improper roads, no perceptions can be accurately made without honesty.

Messages flow in straightforward ways, ever brightening the mind. The mind's electricity flows out and down cascading in pulsating streams, pervading every single cell, joining the melody sung out by waves of life stirring the organism as a whole.

Honesty adds life. Honesty adds joy. Honesty is the only way to spin in harmony with the universe.

Stars and planets, electrons and atoms, molecules and cells, must be trustworthy, incorruptible, incapable of being false, or matter would cease to be, energy would decrease, and coldness and death would replace warmth and light.

"In the beginning there was darkness, but then there was light" and the light is eternal and the eternal light expands into atoms, molecules and stars. It expands in power, in velocity. It has integrity.

Honesty is integrity and when cells lose it they soon shrivel up and die. And when cells lose it, the whole must suffer, too.

Honesty makes for vitality. It makes for beauty and for dreams. It magnifies and blesses, clears the brain, cleanses the emotions, eliminates all strain.

Without honesty there can be no bright tune, nothing accurate, nothing clear. Without honesty, there is frustration, anger and shame, draining emotions for a damaging game.

Maturity requires honesty. Honesty expands the mind into realms of greater being, into levels of greater seeing, more intensive, vital feeling, moving on to joy.

Ask a question. Spark the light. Ask a question! Provoke an answer. Questions are the key to honesty and honesty is the key to fire the soul.

No angry, hating, fearing, no frustrated sneering, hostile person can be honest in his commotion. Honesty means order, clarity and light. Honesty means sensitivity, sensitivity to all of life. It means directness in action and in thought. It means being open to hear the holy sound of the sweetest music that was ever found, of notes of pure pleasure ringing clear and true, the notes of full measure for a life of joy.

Cooperation

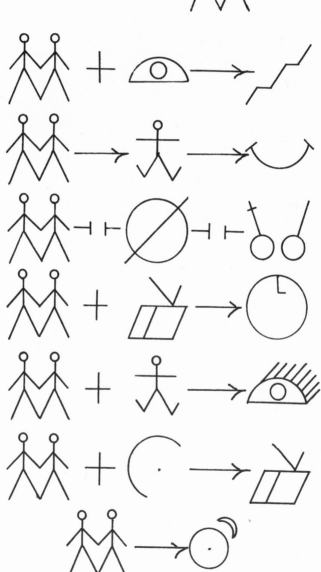

Competition

SONG OF COOPERATION

Beyond the clamor, clash and strain, beyond the pushing and the pain, beyond the competitive strife, there is life. There is life on a higher plane, a level of cooperation, action that is sane.

Competition is a primitive force of collision, of unawareness and of fear. The grabbing, hoarding, shoving—the clamor and all the noise is the result of confusion and inadequacy. The terrifying din hurts all concerned. Energies are wasted. Life is hardly tasted in the confusion of it all.

Cooperation speeds communication, helps the interaction of notes true and pure. It makes for pleasant design in the infinite time of the universe. Cooperation makes for intimacy. It makes for pleasure. It leads to joy. It makes for creation and moves all of life.

When notes merge and then surge into a tune of sweetness and delight, when notes intertwine so true and fine and fill the atmosphere with goodness and with truth, when notes float upwards ever pleasing ever more, that's cooperation. Cooperation is the spontaneous movement together in pleasure. It intensifies delight, brightens and makes cheerful, conquers all that's tearful. It expands our life.

Beyond the cacophony of clanging clamor, beyond the sham and the shame, cooperation greases movement, lends to motion, overcomes the game. The game is a pretense, a fabrication invented by puny men. Life is an inspiration invented solely by God.

Cooperation is the way to insure the distribution of satisfactions aiding in the current flow of life, aiding in the current flow of love, aiding in the flow of blood, flow of urine, flow of power. Cooperation feeds back into the ever expanding concentric circle about the self, moving conscious awareness outward, outward in happy beating waves of love.

Tumbling tongues of tickling flame flare and fly and fuse again. Colors bright fill with fluid warmth moving out beyond the pain, moving out to joy. Cooperation speeds the way.

Brain waves sway in electric excitement moving stronger fed by cooperative powers, fed by honest and efficient usage, fed by working together in harmony made gay.

Brain waves move in vibrant showers indicating emotional states, indicating the moving powers that push on to greater being, finer cooperative ways of intensification, more intricate, exquisite modes of action. Brain waves move and grow stronger fed by cooperation.

The internal and external environments tend to interact. One effects the other. The more cooperation, the faster moves the reaction into more colorful and varied ways, the faster swirl the fluids stirring action into the pattern of happy design.

Altered brain functions alter motor action, change the environment without. Cooperation is a catalytic enzyme exciting actions, interactions, changes all about.

Flickering, flaring, flights of bright vibrations fill full a life with joy. And joy must have cooperation or the tempo is bound to slow.

Competition causes cluster clumps cluttering the distributions of flow. It makes for imbalance, and dumps energies into inconsequential trickles, turning thick and turgid, changing into sludge. Competition exhausts. It makes for suffering and poverty, too.

Cooperation aids the transportation of all nutriment. Cooperation makes for utilization. It makes for efficiency. Cooperation mingles its essence with like essence inspiring the magnetic pulsations moving to and fro and ever out, moving in swifter rhythms greater than those found before. Cooperation mingles and adds its power multiplying what was before into an essence for ever greater movement for creation, movement on to God.

Beams of light and beams of sight, beams of radiance and beams

101

divine, beams of power and beams of joy, beams that tower and beams so fine mingle and intertwine and with cooperation intermix into a varied system of beauty. Cooperation must always be there.

The universe expands shifting towards the red end of the spectrum, pulsating out in streams of stars. Follow the universe. Expand! Move with cooperative effort out. Expand horizons, expand the vision, move in unison out.

As we absorb emissions of joy, emissions that hold together in pleasure, as we absorb radiations of warmth, so we move and expand together.

Cooperation aids perseverence, efforts that lead to accomplishment. Cooperation makes for harmony. Cooperation frees the soul.

Communication flows. It grows. It gains in strength through cooperation. Neural pathways fire electrical discharges in a happy play of messages strengthened and reassured by the excited flow of powers running together.

Molecules and cells discover meaning through their own interplay. Cooperation fills the day with happiness due to the bright expectation of future reactivity. Excitement and stimulation is brought about by cooperation.

Provocation and eventual exhaustion, irritation and scattered flight, those are the symptoms of competition, chasing flickers in the night. The future becomes more darkened, the vision more gray. Dreary days and empty tomorrows drowned with tears and full of sorrows, that's the noise of competition forcing humanity into malnutrition. Coercion and restraint, bitterness and mire, all of them conspire with competition. But all of them are weak, forced to flee away under the warm rays of cooperation.

Beams of joy and beams of light distribute gladness and delight; fill with fullness as we expand to the happy beating heart, fulfilling our expected part in the role of creation. We're just a cog in the scheme, but mightier than we seem, full of infinite power to do, full of force and so unique, full of freedom to react, full of vigor

102

and full of life when we cooperate with the universal surge, the urge to outward movement.

Tongues of tickling, tantalizing streams of multicolored and varied hues shifting, changing from reds to blues and back again, cooperate in one huge adventure, one giant intellectual plan, one great excitation as they cooperate and use their energies in the movement out to life, in the movement out to man, in the movement out to God. Cooperation is the way.

Inneffiency

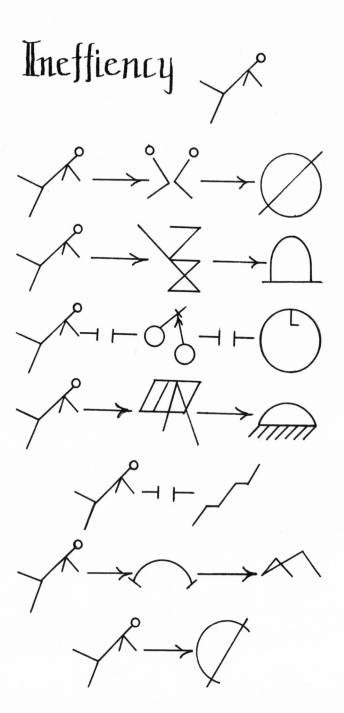

Efficiency

SONG OF EFFICIENCY

Fluids shake and fluids tremble stirred by efficiency. Fluids interact and rumble and whirl about to make a better being. Life is lengthened and strengthened. Refractions and worries tend to decrease.

There are contractions and then relaxations over and over and over again. Repetitive acts are repeated almost the same but yet unique—modified by minute changes, changes for efficiency moving on to greater function, bring to greater abilities, too.

More is done and in less time. More is done and in fun. More and bigger, better and better become the abilities inspired by efficiency—energies conserved and concentrated better and more finely controlled. Vision becomes intensified. Sounds clear and stronger, too. Chemical actions move ever faster, fired by efficiencies and the electro-chemical energies surge forward and merge into a bigger and better organization, a better human being.

Efficiency generates greater powers, forces able to move and do. Efficiency moves to beauty, perfection, better abilities to move and do.

The lights twirl and whirl and become charged into a flurry of power, magnetic force, under the influence of efficiency. They swirl and soar ever straining beyond the limits of the present, moving further into the adventure of a brighter tomorrow, moving ever away from sorrow.

Efficiency lights the path of all creation moving on to swifter, finer, more exact communication, forcing the limits of mortality.

Life extends. The fires roar. The flames shoot up. They soar out. Efficiency lights the way.

Enzymes! Catalysts! Hormones, too! Heart beat, pulse rate, muscles contract and increase in tone. Life glows more intense and perceptions more keen. Efficiency works with honesty and together they clean the lens for viewing the future changing the present into an adventure of joy. Efficiencies overcome all obstructions, all hesitations of fear and hostility. They force clean, swift, honest and open movement together. Efficiencies bring about cooperation, coordination, and construction—movement to delight the heart and the soul—motion to warm the being into the glow of expansion—the glow of humanity.

Efficiency demands change, modification, a brighter future—a better, easier, happier way of action and of thought. Efficiency changes repetitive patterns into yielding, unfolding, evolving designs, plans of greater beauty and goodness, too, ways of originality.

Efficiency upgrades function. It increases the capacity for action. It magnifies energy, strengthening the vibrations, the very strings of being. It speeds the thoughts, opens them wide, sends the electricity out to explore the universe.

It leads to questions and questions lead to answers. Matter? What is matter? Matter is crystallized energy. And energy. What is that? Energy is the capacity for action. Action and interaction, variety and interplay, design and scheme, plan and unfolding. Matter is made of all of that.

Undulations and vibrations, efficiency speeds the waves. Frequencies and pulsations, amplitudes and emanations, efficiency speeds them on. Efficiency increases the utilization of energy.

A better means of distribution, a happier way of transportation, a more joyful way of being, efficiency helps them all. It enters into life's weaving. It's so necessary for intricate design. Every motion, every action, every perception becomes more fine.

Information is easily retrieved under the spell of efficiency. Learning is ever enhanced. The being becomes entranced with the infinite knowledge for living. And the light glows brighter and brighter setting up sympathetic vibrations to fill the atmosphere allowing the energies of the core to penetrate and to unite, to merge and fuse and part again. To fuse and separate each time stronger, brighter, and more efficient than before.

Efficiency is hindered by competition, hindered by fear and strain. Efficiency is hindered by all the forces that call forth pain.

Different emotions form different beings. Varying emotions vary the perceptions. The best call forth efficiency. Pure! Bright! Full of delight! Filled with the joy of light! Filled with the motion of life! Working without deficiency.

Leaping flames intertwine, pulsate up and fill the vision. Dancing powers fuse and form a beating mass of moving structure. Vibrant energies swing about as singing lights blink and shout out a chorus for all living. They all move with efficiency.

Place demands upon the powers. Find it wanting and repeat. Repeat the demands over again. Force an action! Find it wanting and repeat. Repeat! Repeat! Place demands and call forth action and slowly changes appear moving to greater efficiency.

Leaping energies flare greater, pulsating with vigor as they move to the demand of efficiency. The hums of biologic motion accelerate and become more pure, more distinct and more sure. Leaping, falling, leaping again. Never back to the same base line. Something different. Something new. Flowing on. Flowing through. Increased feedback. Increased flow. The lights move brighter and brighter glow.

In the beginning there was nothing. Then vibrations began to move. Sympathetic vital vibrations, vigorous vibrations open to change. Then vibrations began to appear and with it a directed purposeful range of unfolding motion.

Efficiency leads to better coordination, synchronized actions more capable of achievement. It leads to happier methods, methods of action and spontaneous motivation, methods in harmony with Life. Notes of freedom, spontaneous song unfolding, notes of pleasure mingled with thrilling notes of efficiency, form a concert to propel the soul. Once the pattern is established, once deficiency starts being diminished, then the widening cycles unfold entering states of greater meaning, plans of greater seeing, wider being with broad perceiving. Greater choices then appear, more ways of differentiation. Greater abilities appear, more variety and more clear.

Add the fuel of efficiency, holy substance for energy growth. Fire the flight with efficiency. Extend the brightness in the night.

Beyond the perceptive frameworks of men, beyond the sensations honed by pain, are the mystic perceptions of true worth, the perceptions cleared by honesty.

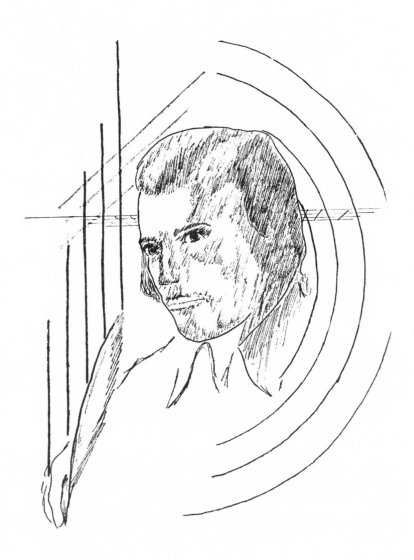

111

Curiosity

Lack of Curiosity

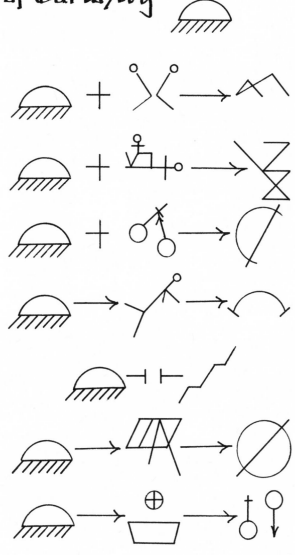

SONG OF IMAGINATION

Imagination is a power for conception, a force for formulations, new creations in interesting and varied ways. Honest imagination moves to God. Dishonest imagination diverts the stream, sullying the dream, pushing the fabric into obscure and sorrow-filled ways.

Honest imagination shines and shimmers, fills with excitement. It causes thirst for adventure, a desire for exploration always moving the core to happy expansion causing an unfolding of the abilities to do.

Imagination structures thoughts and in its creation it structures the world. It changes perceptions, brings conceptions into closer harmony with life. It builds perceptions, intense receptions, into electric currents triggering motion to change, modify and evolve.

Electromagnetic currents surge and spark shaking man's structures, filling the brain with an organization capable of reception of more of the infinite vibratory rays that ring the earth and can fill with mirth and joy those who can perceive.

Imagination is a spark for creation. It sparks the flight of the holy light of the whole. It fuels to infinity our very soul. From the internal currents that flicker and fly forming impressions, changing what the internal eye reveals, come torrents of magnetic currents pouring out upon the external world. And the world changes and the universe does, too.

Imagination, honest imagination clear and clean, sparks all the lights, all the pure vibrations in their flight to unfold, to fulfill, to expand. It's a drive, a current, a power and a source. It propels to creativity.

It adds spice, causes constant variety, forces differentiation, weaves designs of magnificence. Imagination brings brilliant blends of blessed events into relationships.

It causes seeking. It thrills and guides and can be one of the most exciting of the forces, but only when it moves with honesty.

Imagination sparks yearning, fills with a burning desire for solutions. Working with negator elements, it turns the being, disorganizes and misguides. Working with the positive portions, it fuels the flight in colorful roars of song, burst of tones so pure and strong, moving on to life and immortality.

Honest imagination sparks questions, adventures into the unknown. It fills with courage, fills with life, banishes all thoughts of sadness and of pain. It fills with the joy of living.

Imagination is the name of the source of inspiration, a source of wonder and of awe at what God can do. It's a source for reverence, moving human to human, moving humanity to the Divine.

No mechanical objects could be, no rockets could roar for Mars, no telescopes could study the stars without imagination. No problems, great or small, nothing could be solved at all, demanding even the minutest move, without imagination.

It sparks throughts into being, fills them, thrills them, fuses them into schemes for seeing ever more. The electric oscillations form schemes forming dreams that slowly unfold and the world changes.

It helps direct the currents, the energies of life. It helps increase the consciousness of what is all about, extending the range of knowledge and the range of feeling too. It blows hope into being and forces humanity on.

Imagination is the stuff of dreams, the staff of hope and wondrous schemes. It can cast a light even in the bleakest and darkest day. It's the crowning glory for all humanity.

Drums of hope beat happy expectations. Trumpets of adventure blare and thrill the soul. Horns and strings fill the air in holy orchestration of creation. And varied patterns come into being.

Blood and nerves and muscle, too, skin and bone and brain cells, too. Liver, kidney and spleen; once they were an idle dream. Now they form a man. Imagination sparked the way. Honest imagination revealed it.

Imagination is a creation of the mind, an ability to form mental images, structures of thought woven by excitement, electric patterns of a dream. It's the power of invention, a recombination of elements into a more harmonious and pleasing design in tune with the pulsations of the core.

Imagination is an essential to thought. It's necessary for the organization, the structure of this pure energy into waves of perception changing the world as we would want it to be.

Opened up and totally receptive, imagination is able to fire the soul of being into perceiving the will of God. It fills with desire, fills with questions, fills with adventure. It fills with life.

And what is God? The force for life? The force for life! And who is God? The sum total of energy, the sum of all energies. The sum is life.

Imagination fashions answers for excitement, answers for life, answers full of love.

Opened up and totally receptive, moving with honesty, imagination touches inward and unites with the outward too, bringing the soul in contact with God. Light goes flying to light, and expanding all the way. Imagination brings the inner power to the outer power, the inner love to the greatest love. It brings the love of humanity to the love of God.

Imagination brightens the way. And the way is the most important, not the intention to do. The way is vital. The way must be true.

Imagination brings sparkle and infinite delight to the ways of being as the being floods the night questing for joyful union, a union that's divine. It intensifies the love of life and in so doing quickens the beat and brings the love of humanity to the love of God.

The drums of emotion set the beat to being. The trumpets of reason extend the range. The horns of motion push through the ethers. The strings of being move on to life. Imagination fires the way.

Thousands of messages thunder and soar, roar about the earth filling the atmosphere with its music. Millions, billions, trillions of messages bombard our perceptions and what finite number ever come through? How much is seen, felt, heard, smelled or touched? How much is understood?

How many messages do we perceive? How many signals excite the soul? How many waves energize our being? How many vibrations set up hums within us to move us to greater being? How much information enters the brain?

Turn off! Turn on! Tune in! Tune out! A flick of the switch and the mind is closed. A turn of the modifiers and the darkness obscures the light. Another turn and the switch flicks on. The messages come through. The vibrations pour in.

Closed minds, open minds, partially closed, not fully opened—what makes the mind that way? The paired modifiers spin, negative and positive. One side lets light in, intensifies vibrations, increases life. The other side darkens, dampens, deadens and destroys. One side lets the messages in, the other keeps them out. One side charges the forces of being. The other slows the motion. So the paired modifiers spin about the core of being.

But what makes messages stick? What helps us to perceive? What prevents perception once the vibrations do come through?

Organization! We need a framework of information, organization furnished by knowledge and open thoughts. We can't improve our vocabulary unless we understand the language. Without understanding the words have no meaning. They're just a jumble of noise. They may be conveying the most beautiful thoughts but without understanding, we hear only noise.

Open thoughts increase our excitement, extend our knowledge, expand our abilities, increase our being and fill with pleasure. Closed thoughts stop our motion, make for commotion, conflict, confusion and decay. They decrease our pleasure, add to the pain, diminish our perceptions, change life to a game. Closed thoughts assign degrading roles, parts to play always on a much lower level than the crudest life forces would move us to be.

Millions of waves thunder and soar, waves of excitement moving to dance. Millions of signals strive to ignite our souls into energies of expansion pulsating ahead. A flick of the switch and the electricities pour in. But we need honesty, trust, imagination for the task. We need strength to let all the vibrations fill our being. We need crystallized perceptions full of integrity, purity and beauty. We need expectations of pleasure, not pain. We need efficient receptors primed with life, ready to fire us the moment they receive. We need cooperative, highly coordinated systems of being. We need the positive side of every paired modifier that whirls about our core. And then, only then, can we have the strength to flick the switch and let the energies thunder in.

This is the way to mystic being, to vibrations to float the soul. This is the way to enter fresh Life, uncontaminated and unspoiled. He gave us the power to control ourselves, the opportunity to project our souls in flights of infinitely increasing freedom. But we can flick the switch only when the vibrations can echo through. Only when the light of the core can shine through every modifying force, can we charge our souls for the glory flight.

So the soul is fused, fashioned by seven fun-filled flames of fire for sparkling variety. And about the dancing seven suns of internal being, fashioned with infinite intelligence, are the seven double strands interwoven, of the guidance mechanism—a mechanism for attracting and repelling—for keeping on course for the bodies that can react, reason and perceive the fine evolving radiations, the emanations of the holy Light filling with sight and hearing, filling with abilities to respond and care, filling full of love.

The lights revolve and flare, and in the flashing they reveal. Beyond the barriers of body and mind, beyond the dulled emotions and damaged physiology, beyond the structured restricted perceptions of man, are the vibrant uncontaminated vibrations of mystic being. Only receptors oriented to life, primed with honesty and vividly alert, only sensitive receptors so charged with conscious love and hope can catch a glimpse of what it means to be; and flooded with supreme ecstasy be uplifted to the happy expectation for our fetal humanity yet to be born.

Perfect Human